ALFA ROMEO

SPIDER, ALFASUD & ALFETTA GT

Other titles in the Crowood AutoClassics Series

ALFA ROMEO

SPIDER, ALFASUD & ALFETTA GT

The Complete Story

David G. Styles

First published in 1992 by
The Crowood Press Ltd
Ramsbury, Marlborough
Wiltshire SN8 2HR

British Library Cataloguing in Publication Data

A catalogue record for this book is available from the British
Library.

ISBN 1 85223 636 1

Acknowledgements
My sincere thanks are firstly due to Dottore Rinaldo Hercolani,
Director of Press and External Relations at Alfa Romeo's
headquarters in Arese, Milan, as well as to Signora Elvira
Ruocco and Ing Roberto Benvenuti of Alfa Romeo's Centro
Documentazione Storica. I would also thank Father Bernard
Collins for translating some items of text that were only
available in Italian. In addition, my thanks go to: Tim Holmes
and his Press and Public Relations team at Alfa Romeo Great
Britain Limited; to David Vivian of *Autocar & Motor*, to Charles
Pierce and John Herrick of Haymarket Archives for road tests; to
Ian Bond of *Your Classic* magazine and to the National Motor
Museum Picture Library, Beaulieu for colour pictures; and to
Hugh Chevallier. Finally, my thanks go to all those people whose
names do not appear here, but whose help was none the less
invaluable.

Note   Generally speaking, after World War II Alfa Romeo was
not a hyphenated name. Similarly, 'Spider' is spelt in two ways,
with an 'i' and with a 'y'. This is because Pininfarina always
spelt 'Spyder' with a 'y', whereas Alfa Romeo spells it in both
ways. In this book, 'Spider' is spelt as appropriate to the period of
reference.

Dedication
To my wife, Ann, my daughter, Emma, and my son, Philip, for
continuing to tolerate being deserted for a word processor.

Typeset by Avonset, Midsomer Norton, Bath
Printed and bound in Great Britain by BPCC Hazell Books, Aylesbury

Contents

Introduction

I first became aware of Alfa Romeo cars as a small boy, when Giuseppe Farina and Juan Manuel Fangio were the world's leading racing drivers and when Alfa Romeo was *the* name in Grand Prix racing, winning almost every race it entered. It was in those years, too, that I learned of the potential horrors of motor racing, with the cruel twist of fate which ended Achille Varzi's life in an Alfa Romeo 158, during a last practice lap he need not have made for the 1948 Swiss Grand Prix. The sense of honour and respect demonstrated by Alfa Romeo for its own then became apparent and it was this, as much as any other aspect of that company's greatness, which inspired a continuing interest in the cars and affairs of Italy's most notable of car makers.

When I was invited to write this book, I had to think hard about how to link together three such totally different models as the Spider, the Alfetta GT and the Alfasud . . .

Until I realized that all three had the same basic origins. All were born out of the success of Alfa Romeo's Giulietta series of cars. The original 1955 Pininfarina-designed Giulietta Spyder is the first model in the sequence of this story and it was created from the Giulietta Sprint Veloce. As the Giulietta 'grew up', so the Guilia came along, followed by the 1750, then the 2000. The Alfasud was the true small car successor to the Giulietta. Finally, the Alfetta was created.

With all this in mind, I make no apology for describing these cars as real Alfa Romeos, for that is what they truly are. True *Alfisti* must accept that they have a rightful place in Alfa lore and indeed, as you visit any Alfa Romeo club gathering these days, you will find an abundance of two-seaters from Giulietta to Spider, of Alfetta GTs and of Alfasuds and Sprints. If, as you read this book, you are yet undecided, then I hope that it may help you to resolve your indecision.

1 An Introduction to Alfa Romeo

ALFA – THE INSTITUTION

To this day, Alfa Romeo is a name which conjures in the mind visions of a great past, littered with great names and great deeds. And of course, it *does* have a history embellished with racing trophies and lists of victories which are the envy of industry and sport alike. But Alfa Romeo's main aim has always been to manufacture quality cars for sale to its public.

Among the great men who made Alfa Romeo what it was and who laid the foundations of the marque's charisma, were Giuseppe Merosi and Nicola Romeo. It was Merosi's creations which made ALFA, and it was Romeo who built it up into a viable business, with a whole spectrum of business activities. That spectrum, theoretically at least, was the best prospect of being able to survive economic hardships and yet, sadly, it was to cause Romeo's premature retirement, and to take the company on the way to becoming a state-owned industry, albeit one which has always been important to Italy. Because the reputation of Alfa Romeo was, and is, important to Italy, so the names of these two men were important to Alfa Romeo.

This book is concerned with just three lines of a family tree which has many ramifications. Those three are the Spyder, the Alfasud and the Alfetta. At first glance, you could be forgiven for assuming those three lines had nothing at all to do with each other. But all three take their roots in the same successful model, the Alfa Romeo Giulietta.

NEW MARKET – NEW LEGEND

The Giulietta was born of a need for cars in a market place starved of oil and suffering rampant inflation; it was Alfa Romeo's upmarket offering to what it hoped would be a rapidly-expanding band of enthusiasts. The Alfa buyer would be a discerning motorist who knew what he or she wanted; someone who aspired to something better than average or someone who was switching to a smaller car with larger-car performance. All these buyers would be well satisfied with what the Giulietta could offer and indeed, once released upon the world, its sales took off at a rate which alarmed even Alfa Romeo.

The charisma of Alfa Romeo has only ever been eclipsed by one other name, that of Ferrari, and it is open to conjecture whether or not Ferrari would be as well known in the world without Alfa Romeo, for that was where Enzo Ferrari began his climb to success. But Alfa Romeos have always been much more than just expensive cars totally beyond the reach of the enthusiasts. Indeed, Alfa Romeo's greatest enthusiasts have been its owners. Since the terrible devastation of World War II, the Milanese company has worked hard at producing a range of cars which were just above the market average, in quality, performance and price. They have succeeded remarkably well.

Down the years, Alfa Romeo has developed a habit of producing a single version of a new product and selling it as it stood. Often, that original model has not had sparkling

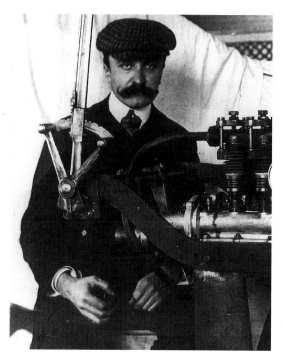

Cavaliere Giuseppe Merosi with his ALFA compressor.

performance, but almost always has shown good manners, and handling qualities better than most of its competition. Once the initial production 'teething troubles' have been eliminated, then the company moves on to enlarge the range and improve the choices available.

It was a slightly different story with the Giulietta. This car was originally offered in two versions, both two-door coupes: the Sprint and the Sprint Veloce, with 65 or 80bhp power outputs—pretty remarkable for their time. Within a few months came the Giulietta Berlina, a family saloon which used the basic engine. And, from this, who possibly could have imagined either the range of cars this new model would develop into, or the proliferation of types it would spawn?

THE FAMILY LINE

It is from here that our family line begins.

Giuseppe Merosi

Giuseppe Merosi was generally credited (correctly) with having breathed life into Anonima Lombarda Fabbrica Italiana. He was endowed with a gentle nature, but a positive sense of direction, combined with a sensitivity for his subject which is difficult to express in English ('Simpatico' has no real equivalent). It was Merosi who set the standard of 'oneness' between car and driver which has been a characteristic of Alfa Romeos ever since.

Born at Piacenza in December 1872, to Giacomo and Anna Merosi, Giuseppe grew up in comfortable circumstances to enter Piacenza Technical Institute, where he graduated as a civil engineering surveyor – a 'Geometra'. During his school and college years, he demonstrated high athletic prowess and was a competent racing cyclist, qualities which would help him in later years in producing machines with which their drivers could easily co-ordinate.

The family business of candle making was abandoned by young Geometra Merosi, as he entered the State Highways Department. He wasn't there for long before he decided, in the mid-1890s, that his enthusiasm for cycling was greater than his enthusiasm for surveying and civil engineering. So, with no more ado, he joined forces with Vittorio Bassi, a mechanical engineer and good friend, to manufacture bicycles under the name 'Ing. Bassi and Merosi', using the trade mark 'Endless'. He went on to OM and Fiat before joining Bianchi in 1906 (where he rose to head of the engineering department), then A.L.F.A. as it was formed in 1910.

Having formally resigned from Alfa Romeo in 1926, after the bankers' shake-up which dislodged Nicola Romeo, Merosi was around the company on and off for many years and his capacity for translating thoughts into engineering drawings was legendary. Indeed, he ended his career as a humble draughtsman at Portello, before dying in near poverty.

The 1750 Spider, a truly beautifully proportioned sports car.

The Giulietta became the most popular Alfa Romeo ever and was produced in greater numbers, in all its forms, than any model before it. But the demand for detail specification improvements here and there increased its weight, so that greater power was needed to maintain the performance. A larger engine therefore came along and, hey presto, the Giulietta had become the Giulia.

The Giulia range rapidly expanded, just as the Giulietta had, and soon it had encompassed all the variations of its smaller forebear, including the Spider in 1,290cc and 1,570cc options. Before anyone had realized it, almost twenty years had passed since the introduction of the Giulietta and, guess what? Yes, it was time to update the range,

having added even diesel engines to the product. The updated cars were the 2000 range, similar in appearance to the Giulias, but mechanically improved and slightly more rounded.

The 2000 was clearly something of a stop-gap, because not long after its release, it was discontinued in favour of a total re-design. In the process of that re-design, it had been decided that a rear-located gearbox, a transaxle, was part of the solution to improving weight distribution, handling and roadholding. The rear suspension was also changed, pretty drastically, with a de Dion rear end and Watts linkage.

So was born the new Alfetta, a historic Alfa Romeo name applied to a volume production

The 1954 Alfa Romeo Giulietta Sprint Coupe.

The Alfa Romeo 2000 Saloon.

car which shared those few rear-end characteristics with its illustrious namesake. This new model came into being with a great flurry of publicity and was accepted in the fashion of its forebears. It started life as an ordinary saloon (as ordinary as any Alfa Romeo saloon has ever been, that is). In now conventional fashion, the Alfetta Saloon was followed by a range of cars, all designed by the man who was to have the styling of several Alfa Romeo models to his credit, Giorgetto Giugiaro.

Given that the 'small car' aspect of Alfa Romeo had been abandoned with development, from 1,290cc to 1,570cc Giulia to 1,750 to 2,000, a need was actually felt at Arese to re-create the Alfa Romeo small car. This came in the form of the Alfasud, with its 1,186cc flat-four engine. And, after its early

teething troubles, it proved to be a worthy successor. The result of the Alfasud's success has only to be witnessed at an Alfa Romeo Owners' Club race meeting in Great Britain, leave alone the number now being renovated as road-going classics.

So, here is our link between these three models of Alfa Romeo. The Spider was born directly out of the Giulietta design and has a continuous history of development behind it. The Alfasud, also designed by Giorgetto Giugiaro, was the return to the small car, so owing much to the success of the Giulietta for its very conception. Then we have the Alfetta, which was the direct heir to the Giulietta's success story. Thus they are all closely related, despite being quite different: all heirs to the 'Genus Alfa' and all part of the same success story.

Revival of a name – the Alfetta – this is a 1.8 family saloon endowed with some of the characteristics of a Grand Prix single-seater.

The original Alfasud Saloon of 1972.

Alfa 33 Boxer 16V.

Full frontal of the Alfa Romeo SZ Type ES30.

The Alfa Romeo badge of today.

Giovanbattista Razelli, Chief Executive of Alfa Lancia SpA.

The Alfa Romeo Badge

The design of the Alfa-Romeo badge is a story in itself but, briefly, it is an adaptation of the arms of the Visconti family, who held the Duchy of Milan. That family had its origins in the fifth century AD and its founder, Umberto of Angera, is reputed to have slain a serpent which roamed the area, devouring humans. So the coat of arms of the Viscontis became a serpent with a human in its mouth. Between the tenth and thirteenth centuries, the Visconti and other Lombardy families sent an army to the Christian Crusades against the might of Islam, so added a red cross on a white background to the coat of arms. When Francesco Sforza assumed the title of Duke of Milan, he built the magnificent Castello Sforza and above the Great Door had his coat of arms inset for all to see.

Giuseppe Merosi, shortly after the formation of A.L.F.A. in 1910, was asked to look for a suitable emblem as a badge for the new company. He did no more than pass the task down to a young draughtsman, Romano Cattaneo, whose brother Giustino was at that time a prominent designer with Isotta Fraschini. Young Romano was waiting one morning at the Piazza Castello tram terminus, looking around and day-dreaming as he waited for his transport to work at Portello. Suddenly, the coat of arms above the Great Door caught his eye and he had his badge! Out of respect to the Viscontis and the City, the shield became a disc and the two halves of the badge were transposed, the dragon moving to the right. A blue circle was placed around the serpent and cross and within it was inscribed the letters 'A.L.F.A.' in the top half and 'Milano' in the lower half, with a Savoia knot on left and right of the circle to separate the words. After Nicola Romeo's acquisition of the company, the words 'Alfa-Romeo' replaced 'A.L.F.A.' in the top half of the badge and that, in slightly modified form is how the badge stands today.

Nicola Romeo

Nicola Romeo was the man who gave A.L.F.A. the chance to survive and, of course, the other half of its name. He was born at San Antimo, in the province of Naples in April 1876, to a family of humble means. To his great credit, he graduated from Naples Technical Institute to receive his Engineer's Licence in 1889. With a continuing thirst for knowledge, Romeo went to work in Belgium and studied at Liège for a second degree, this time in electrical engineering. Gaining work experience in Belgium, France, England and Germany, he returned to Italy in 1902, settling in Milan.

In that same year, Nicola Romeo established himself as an agent for Ingersoll Rand tools and equipment. His business flourished and in 1911, he formalized the business, by setting up Accomandita Ingegnere Romeo & C. at number 10, Via Ruggeri di Lauria in Milan. Now he added the product ranges of Blackwell and Hadfield to his portfolio, as well as manufacturing mining equipment. With the onset of the Great War, Romeo's engineering capacity was much in demand and his business expanded rapidly, so much so that he was able, when it fell on hard times, to acquire the business of A.L.F.A. and add its manufacturing capacity to his own.

Nicola Romeo had much to do with the creation of the Alfa Romeo legend in his own lifetime and it was down to his management of the company that Alfa Romeo won the World Grand Prix Championship in 1925. It was Nicola Romeo who authorized the development of the P2 and it was he who took the company into the serious business of winning races and making aero engines.

Ingegnere Nicola Romeo, founder of the name 'ALFA ROMEO'.

TODAY – TOMORROW

Even as this book is being written, the story continues, for the 1991 season saw the Alfa Romeo Spider continuing in production, extensively face-lifted and mechanically updated, but essentially the same car for all that. Instead of the Alfasud, today we have the Alfa 33; some might say the Alfasud grown up, and they would be right in some degree, for the Alfasud, through the 33, has followed the same path as the Giulietta, becoming a slightly larger car with a larger power unit. And whilst the Alfetta GT became the GTV-6, it faded for a while, with no immediate successor. That was before the limited edition Tipo ES30, otherwise known as the SZ. But then came the Alfa 164 Coupe, created in the same idiom as the SZ, but with four-wheel drive. This is the first four-wheel-drive Alfa 'Super Car', and though not destined for production, is a revelation of things to come.

With the exception only of the Spider (and that may change by the end of 1993), it appears that the grand plan for Alfa Romeo

The ES 30.

is to have front- or four-wheel drive throughout its range of models. It is forecast that the successor to the 75 will feature four-wheel drive and will inherit some of the SZ's adventurous styling in its new, more rounded shape.

After the Alfa Romeo Sprint, we simply had to wait. This magnificent little car, very much underrated before the 1.7 version came along, has now gone. The engine lives on in the 33 and a new three-door low-line sporty coupe may be around the corner, in the form of an Alfa 33 Sprint. If it were to be built in four-wheel-drive form then it would be a thoroughly exciting car in the true Alfa Romeo tradition. And, of course, we *do* have the four-cam, four-valve-per-cylinder flat-four engine, which provides 137bhp to pull along these magnificent Alfa 33s in all their forms.

Ingegnere Giovanbattista Razelli, currently Chief Executive of Alfa Lancia SpA, has hinted in recent press interviews at various possibilities for the short-term future of Alfa Romeo. One thing is certain about Signor Razelli's predictions. After ten years as General Manager at Ferrari, he will have learned that you only make predictions when you can substantiate them. And with the declared intention on record of taking Alfa Romeo into a higher profile international arena, watch out for more exciting new models in the not-too-distant future . . .

2 From Little Acorns –
A.L.F.A. to Alfa Romeo

Anonima Lombarda Fabbrica Automobili was formed in the year 1910, as the direct consequence of the demise of Darracq in Italy. Alexandre Darracq had established the Italian branch of his company in Naples during February 1905. However, by the end of the year, it was realized that the distance between Suresnes, in France, and Naples was too great for the enterprise to enjoy the support it needed to survive. A new site was therefore secured for Societa Anonima Italiana Darracq at Portello, near to Milan,

An example of the Darracq 2-cylinder car manufactured in Italy. There is a restored example in the Alfa Romeo Museum at Arese.

The first ALFA model, a 24hp with Giuseppe Merosi and his family aboard.

in the north of Italy. Recession in the motor industry during 1908, combined with poor quality components delivered from France, saw the end of Italian Darracq in 1909 and the birth of A.L.F.A. a year later. Alexandre Darracq tried hard to prevent his business from sinking, but the Italian banks were to thwart his efforts.

A small group of enthusiastic motorists made an approach to the Banca Agricola d'Italiana, which had been one of the institutions to help fund the Darracq concern. The prospect of easing its own burden doubtless motivated the Bank to provide a loan of 500,000 Lire. This funding was enough to acquire and liquidate the Darracq business to start anew with the formation of Anonima Lombarda Fabbrica Automobili, under the managing directorship of Ugo Stella and the engineering leadership of a civil engineer, Geometra (Surveyor) Giuseppe Merosi – the man who can truly be said to have set the foundations of one of Italy's greatest automotive legends: Alfa Romeo.

MEROSI CREATES THE FIRST ALFA

Giuseppe Merosi came to A.L.F.A. from the motor firm Bianchi, where he had already proved he was no engineering slouch, despite having no mechanical engineering training as such. Merosi had graduated at Piacenza and, in the mid-1890s, decided to go for cycling rather than for surveying and civil engineering. He joined forces with Vittorio Bassi, a mechanical engineer and good friend, to manufacture bicycles under the name 'Ing. Bassi and Merosi', using the trade mark 'Endless'. He went on to OM and Fiat before joining Bianchi in 1906.

As far as A.L.F.A. was concerned, Merosi's background was good enough for Ugo Stella and he was given the job of creating a new all-Italian car out of the ashes of Darracq's failure. His first range of engines were all four-cylinder types, though the first ALFA cars built at Portello were based on the earlier two-cylinder Darracq, simply as a means of putting something into production.

These four-cylinder cars began with the 24hp, a four-litre side-valve engined car, the prototype of which carried a four-seat touring body. From this car was developed the first-ever purpose-built ALFA racing car, described as a two-seat Spider – though it was the 40/60hp model which scored their first victory and which campaigned in the 1914 Coppa Florio. With third and fourth places in that race under their belts, the mighty reputation of ALFA had begun, but the 'Romeo' element was yet to become involved. As ALFA faced its first financial crisis, Nicola Romeo came on to the scene in the early days of the Great War of 1914–18.

ENTER NICOLA ROMEO

Early in 1915, the infant ALFA found itself desperately short of funds. A civil and electrical engineer named Nicola Romeo was the man who came to the rescue. He had held franchises for several famous construction equipment names, including Blackwell, Ingersoll-Rand and Hadfield.

This was the year that Italy entered the Great War and at that time, Romeo was manufacturing an air-compressor named 'The Little Italian' and wanted to expand his business. So, in December 1915, he acquired ALFA's assets from the Banca di Sconto and in February 1918, re-named the Company 'Societa Anonima Italiana Ingegnere Nicola

The 24hp engine in stationary form.

Giuseppe Campari beside the 40–60hp racing car at the 1920 Parma-Berceto Hill-Climb.

Romeo & C'. Now, Giuseppe Merosi was given the task of producing a new range of cars under the Alfa-Romeo badge.

Merosi's first post-war car, the G1, a large limousine which owed much to the studies its designer had made of contemporary luxury cars, was not really what the market place wanted, so the pre-war 20/30 and 40/60 models returned to production while the Company was re-organized. Part of that re-organization was to go the credit of a young man who was employed as a test driver. His name was Enzo Ferrari and through him, a designer of great natural talent was recruited to Alfa Romeo – Vittorio Jano.

Jano's success with the P2 racing car had brought Alfa Romeo the World Grand Prix Championship and with it a fresh introduction to the world of aviation. The Italian government, impressed with the company's

achievements, approached Nicola Romeo (who himself was no stranger to government contracts) to ask if he would undertake the licence manufacture of a British aero engine for the Regia Aeronautica. The engine was the 420hp Bristol Jupiter nine-cylinder radial.

However, 1925 was a bad year commercially for Alfa-Romeo, for so much attention had been given to achieving racing success that cars had not been sold in sufficient quantities to meet the company's costs. So, when the Banca Nazionale di Sconti was wound up in late 1925, Alfa-Romeo's banking affairs were taken over by a consortium of other bankers, who instructed a major re-organization to take place.

In consequence of the changes, Nicola Romeo was replaced as president of the company by Ugo Ojetti, whose principal

An Alfa-Romeo built Bristol 'Jupiter' aero engine.

claim to success hitherto had been as a writer. The situation had not been helped by the Italian government's invitation to Alfa-Romeo to manufacture aero engines. It was an invitation they felt they could not refuse, as it was an honour to be chosen to do such valuable government work, but the tooling costs and setting up did little for the company's financial state. Alfa Romeo had also taken on railway work in the form of manufacturing diesel locomotives, and they had also begun a line of marine engines.

THE NEW DECADE AND NEAR COLLAPSE

Despite further government contracts for aero engine work, including the seven-

Produced between 1920 and 1925, this Alfa-Romeo powered shunting locomotive had a diesel engine, demonstrating the forward thinking typical of the Milanese company.

cylinder Armstrong-Siddeley Lynx, the uncertainties of the early 1930s visited themselves upon Alfa-Romeo, just as they did upon almost the whole world, in consequence of the disastrous 1929 Wall Street Crash. Much of Alfa-Romeo's production capacity was now taken up with the manufacture of the aircraft engines they had licenced, as well as developing their own in-line light aero engines, having taken over the Colombo concern. Simply, their product base was far too wide.

During 1932, the Alfa Romeo board decided that the privately owned dealers were not achieving sufficient business and established a chain of factory branches throughout the country. As a result of the enormous pressure this decision placed on Alfa Romeo's resources, Milan was shaken by the news that the company could not continue trading without outside help.

Fortunately, Benito Mussolini had, earlier

Ugo Gobbato, Director General of Alfa Romeo between 1933 and 1945.

Ugo Gobbato

Ugo Gobbato was born in July 1888 at Volpago del Montello, a little to the north of Venice, the son of a modest landowner/farmer. Studying at Treviso Technical Institute, he secured a Technical Licence and, after working to earn enough money to go back to school, he studied electrical and mechanical engineering at Vicenza. Then he moved to Germany, taking employment as a draughtsman whilst he worked for his Mechanical and Electrical Engineering degrees at Zwickau. After working for Marelli, Gobbato entered the Italian Army for the rest of the war in 1916, where he gained experience in aviation engineering and planning, as he was given the job of re-organizing an aircraft factory in Florence.

Ugo Gobbato was an efficient operator, who returned from the Great War to work with Fiat. His first major task there was to equip the then-new Lingotto factory with all its tools and equipment for the manufacture of motor vehicles and, in 1923, when Benito Mussolini visited Lingotto, Gobbato was assigned to escort him round the factory. Mussolini was impressed with Gobbato and said so, with the result that a few years later, Gobbato was seconded to NSU in Germany to re-organize that business. This was followed by another foreign assignment, this time to Spain to organize Fiat Espana. After that, he was seconded to Moscow, with the difficult task of setting up the Riv ball-bearing factory. After two years, he returned to Italy and Alfa Romeo.

Having restructured the company and made it an efficient manufacturing machine, Gobbato gave everything he had to the success of Alfa Romeo and the safety of its employees during the dark days of World War II. His reward was the accusation of collaboration with the Germans, a charge of which he was completely cleared. Even so, whilst walking to his office on the morning of 28 April 1945, he saw a blue Lancia Agusta stop nearby. He waved to the occupants, whom he clearly knew. Two of them stepped out of the car and shot him where he stood. Italy had lost a true patriot. Alfa Romeo had lost a leader and a brilliant mind.

in that same year, instructed the formation of a government body to assist, or even take into State ownership, companies seen to be of national importance which ran into difficulties. This was the Istituto Ricostruzioni Industriale (IRI). Now Mussolini was an Alfa Romeo user and so saw it as a matter of national pride that the company should be saved. So Alfa-Romeo was taken over by the IRI and reshaped to give it a better opportunity of returning to commercial success.

With the re-organization of Alfa Romeo came new management and on the 1st of December, the IRI appointed Ugo Gobbato as Director General. Gobbato had recently returned from the Soviet Union, where he had been responsible for setting up the Riv ball-bearing factory in Moscow. Two years in the Russia of those days had taken its toll of

him and his family, but when the IRI approached Gobbato with the offer of his dreams, he snatched it with both hands and set about trying to salvage the chaos of Alfa Romeo.

Gobbato's Alfa Romeo appointment was almost certainly instigated by Mussolini himself. The latter had already declared his feelings about the company in the discussions which preceded the IRI's take-over in favour of Fiat's suggested absorption into the O.M. Division of that empire. Gobbato quite deliberately set about restructuring Alfa Romeo into an industrial machine to produce aero and marine engines, trucks and buses, as well as heavy forges and railway equipment. Cars and motor racing were determined to be the 'public relations tool', the bit that kept the public aware of Alfa Romeo's existence, but

Alfa Romeo Tipo 500 trucks on the production line at Portello in 1938/39.

certainly not the bit that paid the company's way.

With the likely onset of war in Ethiopia and civil war looming even larger in Spain, Ugo Gobbato's decision on the company's future products was seen to be a wise one. There was bound to be considerable government work for Alfa Romeo out of those two events, quite apart from the fact that he had vast experience upon which to draw. So the company gave less time and attention to the motor car, with the result that Vittorio Jano, unhappy with the change of direction, began to lose ground in the Alfa Romeo power base.

REINFORCING THE TEAM

During 1936, Ugo Gobbato decided that his engineering team needed greater strength, especially in the field of aero engine design. So, when his old acquaintance, Wifredo Ricart, popped up in Milan at the start of the Spanish Civil War (by some strange coincidence), he was immediately engaged by Gobbato, initially as a consultant designer. Ricart was a very thorough engineer, endowed with a tremendously innovative mind and lots of experience of aero engines and Grand Prix cars. He was clearly the right man to sort out Alfa Romeo's technical problems, and that is exactly what he did, even though he was still only a consultant.

By 1938, with the acquisition and absorption of Scuderia Ferrari, Gobbato was well on the way to having both completed his restructure of Alfa Romeo and to having solved most of its current management problems. Sadly, 1938 was also the year in which Nicola Romeo died, at the age of seventy-three. He had seen his company pass through many trials and had given it his all.

The two greatest innovative achievements of Wifredo Ricart's Alfa Romeo career were an aero engine and a Grand Prix car, both

Wifredo Ricart's aviation masterpiece, the 28-cylinder turbocharged Tipo 1101 aero engine.

startling designs of their time. Perhaps it was because they were both 'on the leading edge of technology' that neither went further than the prototype stage. The aero engine was the Type 1101, a 28-cylinder four-row liquid-cooled radial which, in 1942, produced 2,000hp. In fact, it is too simple to describe it as a 'four-row radial', since it actually consisted of seven four-cylinder in-line engines mounted around a common crankshaft. One of these was later re-designed into a four-cylinder marine engine and put into production. The other magic Ricart creation was a rear-engined 1.5-litre racing car, the Tipo 512, which employed two-stage supercharging to produce the amazing power output, for its time and with a 1.5-litre capacity, of 335bhp at 8,600rpm – almost 200bhp per litre!

Ricart credited these amazing power outputs very largely to the use of centrifugal superchargers. The Type 1101 aero engine had a huge rear-mounted centrifugal blower, whilst the flat-twelve engine of the 512 was designed with a centrifugal first-stage supercharger feeding two Roots-type units,

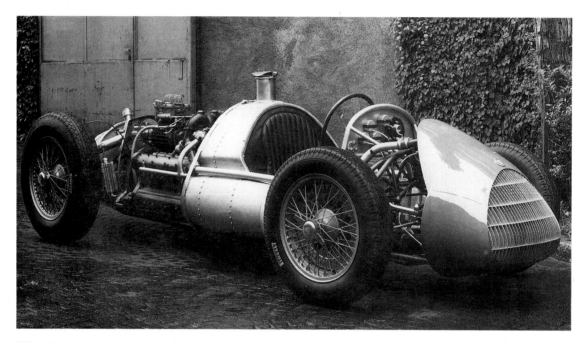

Ricart's racing masterpiece which never raced, but what a car! Here it is, the Tipo 512 Grand Prix chassis, undressed.

one to each bank of cylinders. However, when the car was finally built, it had only a pair of Roots superchargers, one slightly larger than the other, the two working as first and second stages.

WAR, THEN PEACE

As war closed in on Italy, so Alfa Romeo ceased building cars. The latter were replaced by aero engines, aircraft propellors, trucks, buses and marine engines. As with most companies in their position, when opportunity presented itself, there was the occasional moment of development on cars. During that war, the Portello factory suffered three direct hits, the last one, in October 1944 (after Italy had surrendered), causing extensive damage. Finally, the war ended and the company returned to the manufacture of peacetime products, though materials were in desperately short supply.

Words are not necesary for this wartime advertisement for the Alfa Romeo Marine diesel.

The major post-war success of Alfa Romeo's engineering policy lay in the hands of a young man who was groomed by Wifredo Ricart. Indeed, he was Ricart's personal secretary for a time and then was placed in charge of research and calculations in the Servizio Studi Speciale, the Special Projects Department. This young man was Dr Orazio Satta Puliga, who was ably supported by another young engineer, Giuseppe Busso. These two worked closely together and led the design team which produced the 1900 Series and the smaller Giulietta which followed it into production.

Alfa Romeo was now set for a period of considerable success and its car range flourished. So did the other products for which it achieved notable success, including trucks and aero engines. But our attention here is concentrated on the development of the car business and, in the late 1950s, with the birth of the European Common Market, the factory site at Pomigliano d'Arco was put to the manufacture of Renault cars under licence. This was the second time in Alfa Romeo's history that one of its factories had been used for the production of French cars, calling to mind the very origins of the company, when it was itself born out of the old French Darracq company.

The Renault project was quite successful and gave Alfa Romeo the experience it needed in true mass production to move ahead towards its next goal: a small high-volume car of its own design to take up where the original Giulietta had left off. But this diversion to Pomigliano d'Arco gave Alfa Romeo another opportunity, that of building a brand new manufacturing facility at Arese, north-west of Milan, to ease the pressure on the old Portello, which was now bursting at the seams. As the new Arese factory was completed, so the company also established a magnificent new vehicle proving ground of its own at Balocco, reproducing all kinds of road conditions imaginable.

France's Renault Dauphine became the 'Ondine' when manufactured by Alfa Romeo.

The 1983 Alfasud TI Saloon, now a three-door hatchback.

NEW CONSTRUCTION, NEW DIRECTIONS

Ultimately, the factory site destined for Alfa Romeo's new small saloon car was Pomigliano d'Arco and the car which was to emerge from it was the Alfasud. The product of Rudolf Hruska's brilliant mind, the Alfasud immediately betrays the background of its creator, using as it does a flat-four 'Boxer' engine. It was an immediate success, but apart from the fact that the car was Hruska's, and Alfa Romeo's, most adventurous project to date, it was Hruska, too, who was responsible for the creation of the new factory built at Pomigliano d'Arco for the manufacture of the Alfasud.

Moving on, Arese saw the introduction of

the Alfetta Saloon, which was to replace the Giulia Series, now rather long in the tooth and beginning to lose sales. These two products, the Alfasud and Alfetta, were to be the mainstay of Alfa Romeo's business for several years, although a smaller saloon reviving the name of Giulietta was produced alongside the Alfetta.

The Ford Capri revived the sporting aspirations of many a young family man, who hankered after a sports car, but now had a wife and the European standard 2.2 kids, because it gave him the *impression* of driving a sports car, with the *appearance* of a sports car, all wrapped up in what was essentially a two-door family saloon. This created a market niche that not even the mighty Ford could fill, so half the car makers in the world

Wifredo Ricart during a test-drive session with the Tipo 316 Grand Prix Car.

Wifredo Ricart

Born in May 1897 at Barcelona, Wifredo Ricart (the 'L' was actually never there originally, it has been added by all who wrote about him since) came from an old Catalàn family. After graduating in Barcelona, he went on to set up his own engineering business, which led him to the design and manufacture of cars. It was this engineering business, Las Fabricas Ricart y Espana Reunidas, which first brought him into contact with Ugo Gobbato, when Ricart was called upon by the Spanish Government to assist with the creation of Fiat Espana. Ricart had also manufactured his own car, but it failed to make the limelight — slightly surprisingly, perhaps, in view of his recognized highly innovative talent.

Ricart joined Alfa Romeo in 1936, having fled his native Spain as the Civil War erupted. He was almost instantly engaged as a consultant by Alfa Romeo and quickly made his mark. Apart from his own creations, a V-8 and 28-cylinder aero engines, the Types 162 and 512 racing cars, Ricart created stability and regenerated curiosity in the engineering departments of Alfa Romeo, both of which were essential to creative engineering. However, he made adversaries, too, in the form of Vittorio Jano and Enzo Ferrari. Jano resented Ricart's arrival, most probably as he felt it was the cause of his eventual displacement, whilst Ferrari despised Ricart simply because he was a serious threat, even though it was that very threat which cast the die of Ferrari's whole future thereafter.

After World War II, Wifredo Ricart returned to his native Spain and, among his great achievements, added the creation of the V-8 Pegaso Grand Touring car to his list of design credits.

The highly successful Alfetta GT Coupe.

latched on to the fashion and began to offer something similar.

Alfa Romeo was not going to lose ground to this market sector and set about creating two particular cars, of totally different characteristics, to fill their share of that market. Both new cars were to be low-slung four-

seaters, one with rear-wheel drive in the Alfetta family and the other to be front-wheel drive in the Alfasud family. Thus were born the Alfetta GT and the Alfasud Sprint in the mid-1970s. The charisma gained from these two models is often underestimated, but there is no doubt that they helped give

Alfa Romeo a boost when their image wasn't too strong.

When it came to replacing the Alfasud, the Company found itself strapped for cash, so a deal was struck with an oriental manufacturer, in the fashion of the day, to co-produce a new car. The partner was the Japanese giant, Nissan, and the car was to be the ARNA (Alfa-Romeo–Nissan Auto). The joint venture was located in a new factory at Avellino but, sadly, the public reaction to the Arna was poor. As a consequence, the Arna

was finally abandoned and Alfa Romeo was forced to go to its paymasters, the IRI, for help.

In the new European commercial spirit of the mid-1990s, the IRI asked first if there was not a company somewhere that would buy Alfa Romeo. This would save the government the problem of the capital expenditure essential to taking the company into the 1990s. A fierce battle ensued between Ford and Fiat, though it was almost predictable that if Fiat came up with a deal

The second series Alfa 33 Saloon 1.7.

*Successor to the Alfasud, here was the Alfa Romeo/Nissan co-production
known as the Arna, this is a 1.2L.*

which was acceptable to the government, there was no chance of the name 'Alfa Romeo' slipping out of Italian hands. After all, to many, Italian motoring *was* and *is* Alfa Romeo.

ALFA-LANCIA AND FIAT

So today, Alfa Romeo advances as a component of the Fiat empire, remaining an individual marque under the label of Alfa-Lancia, with many Lancia cars flowing out of its doors, to use to the best effect the factory space at Arese. Alfa Romeo's flagship, the 164, was conceived before Fiat's take-over and was allowed to progress. It has proved to be an outstanding car.

The Alfa 75, introduced in 1985, continues to sell well and also has a popular image, whilst the Alfa 33, another successor to a proud name of the past, has recently been face-lifted and fitted with a 137bhp four-cam 1,712cc 'Boxer' engine for its top-of-the-range model. Alfa Romeo looks set fair to enter the twenty-first century with its head held high, though we have yet to learn what are to be the successors to the Alfa Romeo Sprint and Alfetta Coupes, as the Spider continues on . . .

3 The Alfa Romeo Legend

NEW CREATIONS

First of the new product range built at Portello, after the transfer of Darracq's interests to ALFA, was the 24hp: a side-valve four which grew into the 20/30. This was followed by Giuseppe Merosi's 15/20hp design and the 40/60hp, the latter being a pushrod-operated overhead valve engine. In these earliest days of ALFA, Giuseppe Merosi introduced the famous emblem of Alfa Romeo down the years – the *Quadrifoglio* (the four-leaf clover). It was first incorporated into the plate which carried the engine and chassis numbers to identify the

car. It wasn't long afterwards that the *Quadrifoglio* became symbolic of ALFA's racing success, and today almost anyone would tell you it was the emblem of Alfa Corse, the factory racing team.

In those same early days, Merosi recruited to ALFA two men he knew from his days at Bianchi. Antonio Santoni, also a surveyor by training, was a brilliant draughtsman and a thoroughly competent mechanical engineer. He left Bianchi before Merosi, to join the ill-fated Darracq, where he patented a mechanically driven centrifugal supercharger as early as 1910. Nino Franchini was the other new recruit to ALFA, having

ALFA's first true racing machine, the 24hp Corsa (Racer) of 1912/13.

The 20/30 ES Sports four-seater Tourer.

One of Italy's first aeroplanes, the Santoni-Franchini Biplane with Alfa 24hp engine.

gained a reputation as a racing driver with Bianchi.

These two bright young men paired up in 1910 to create one of Italy's earliest rigid airframed aeroplanes which, because he was impressed with the design, Ugo Stella allowed to be completed in the ALFA workshops. The Santoni-Franchini biplane was powered by a 24hp ALFA engine and was the first truly all-Italian aircraft to fly a noteworthy distance. It went on to serve as a trainer at Milan's Taliedo Airport and remained there for some years, after which it seems to have disappeared.

Motoring was ALFA's main purpose in life, though, and in 1911, in keeping with the fashion of proving cars by competing them, ALFA fielded two cars in the sixth Targa Florio race, driven by Franchini and Ronzoni. Neither car finished but, undaunted, Merosi entered a single car in the 1913 Targa, which also failed to finish. However, the 1913 Parma-Berceto Hill Climb was a

different story. Here, Franchini, driving a 40/60, finished second only to Marsaglia's Aquila-Italiana. A year later, in 1914, Giuseppe Campari and Nino Franchini were third and fourth in the gruelling Coppa Florio.

The first post-war car which came out of Portello was far from a sports car. In fact, it was the Type G1, a large six-cylinder engined limousine, one example of which became Nicola Romeo's personal transport. But sporting cars were not to be held down, so the pre-war 20/30 and 40/60 models returned to the forefront, driven by such famous men as Giuseppe Campari, Antonio Ascari and Ugo Sivocci. The sporting tradition of Alfa Romeo had begun in earnest.

It was during this same period that another name emerged to enhance the Alfa Romeo image and set in motion another story. That name was Enzo Ferrari. *Il Cavallino Rampante* adorned many of Alfa-Romeo's

The magnificent Tipo G1 in Coupe de Ville form.

Campari and Fugazza pose aboard the 40/60hp with which they came third in the 1921 Targa Florio.

racing successes between 1929, when Scuderia Ferrari was formed to race on behalf of the works, and 1938, when 'Alfa-Corse' was re-formed to bring the racing activity back under factory control.

THE FIRST ALFA-ROMEOS

The first car to be designed as an Alfa-Romeo (as distinct from A.L.F.A.) was the Type RL, a 3-litre car which was produced as a Sports or Normal chassis. Later came the Targa Florio version, which was the first racing car to bear the *Quadrifoglio* emblem as the symbol of Alfa-Corse. Thanks to a Grand Prix formula which called for a 2-litre engine capacity limit from 1923, Alfa Romeo then concentrated more attention on building cars with small engines, commencing with the Grand Prix Type P1, which was to make its

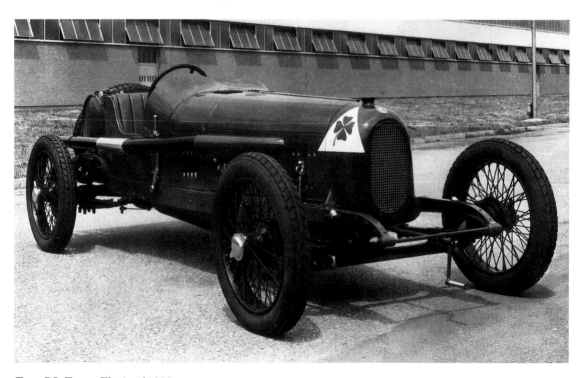

Type RL Targa Florio of 1923.

debut at the Italian Grand Prix in September. However, Ugo Sivocci lost his life in a P1 whilst testing before the race, with the result that the team was withdrawn from that race. The P1 was never fielded in competition after that, though one car was fitted with a supercharger for development.

The design work spent on the P1 was not wasted, though, for a new young engineer, said to have been poached from Fiat by Enzo Ferrari, was given the task of studying the P1 and designing a successor. That young man was Vittorio Jano, one of Italy's greatest-ever racing car designers. The new car was the legendary P2 Alfa-Romeo, powered by a 2-litre twin overhead camshaft fitted with a roller bearing crankshaft and a

Enzo Ferrari in 1927, at the wheel of an Alfa 1500SS.

Enzo Ferrari

Before the Great War, Enzo Ferrari frequented the bars around Monza where the fast and famous drank, with the result that he came to know most of the prominent racing drivers of the time. One of them was Ugo Sivocci, then chief tester for CMN, an Italian motorcycle manufacturer, who took a liking to Ferrari and took him 'under his wing'.

A sequence of sad events befell Enzo Ferrari around this time. His father died from pneumonia in 1916 and a few months later, he lost his brother Alfredo, who had been invalided from the army. In 1917, seemingly alone, the young Enzo joined the army himself, but was seriously ill late in 1918 and was transferred to a hospital for hopeless cases, clearly expected to die. However, he recovered and towards the end of the war was discharged from the army, apparently now qualified as a mechanic and armed with a letter of introduction from his commanding officer to the Fiat company. Ferrari's application for employment there was rejected and so he took a job as a delivery driver, conveying war surplus vehicles between Turin and Milan.

In 1920, Ferrari went to Alfa-Romeo as a test driver and seemingly was considered quite competent. It is said that when a vacancy arose for the position of chief test driver, Ferrari nominated his old mentor, Ugo Sivocci, who accepted the position. Since racing drivers were selected from the ranks of test drivers. Ferrari's prospects were now much improved. Whilst not an outstanding racing driver, he did not lack courage or stamina. Indeed, when he won the 1923 Circuit of Savio race at Ravenna, he was presented with the emblem borne by Italy's outstanding Great War air ace, Count Francesco Baracca, a graduate of the Monza Military Academy.

This connection came about because Alfredo Ferrari, Enzo's brother, served under Baracca in the same squadron and, since Alfredo died after serving his country, Baracca's mother felt that the courage of the Ferrari family, manifested in Enzo, should be recognized by the gift of the emblem. That emblem was a black prancing horse, which Ferrari enclosed in a yellow shield (Modena's adopted colour), capped with the red, white and green of Italy's tricolour flag. Those colours are instantly recognizable today as the 'Cavallino Rampante', but without Alfa Romeo, Enzo Ferrari might simply have been another young hopeful who was lost in the oblivion of mediocrity.

As it was, Ferrari went on to establish a great reputation as a team manager and, ultimately, one of Italy's most famous manufacturers of cars.

Vittorio Jano

Vittorio Jano is generally considered to have been one of the outstanding design engineers of his time. Yet he was not a graduate of any important Technical Institute or University. Born in 1891 at Turin, he went to work with Ceirano in 1904, at the age of fifteen, where he served a kind of apprenticeship.

Still only twenty years old, Jano went to Fiat in 1911 and was engaged as a draughtsman under the direction of Carlo Cavalli. There, he worked hard and enjoyed the respect of his peers as a young man capable of great ingenuity. In those days, Fiat was still involved in motor racing and Jano finally found a way to become involved in the racing programme.

In 1923, Enzo Ferrari was building up his team at Alfa Romeo and had the ear of Giuseppe Merosi. He knew Jano and respected the work he had done on Fiat's 805 and 405 engines, so mentioned his name to Merosi. As a result, in October 1923, Vittorio Jano joined Alfa Romeo, with the first task of taking the P1 Grand Prix car and making a success of it. The result was the instant and outstanding success called the P2. This set Jano on his way with Alfa Romeo and he rose to become Technical Director.

However, with the arrival of Ugo Gobbato, the increasingly expanding range of design tasks and the fact that he was personally overstretched, Jano began to fall short of his and Alfa Romeo's objectives. The result was that this brilliant engineer was finally removed from his high office and placed in a lower position under, of all things, a Spaniard. Jano finally left Alfa Romeo to become Technical Director of Lancia, where his stock rose again. Sadly, believing he had an incurable disease (he probably did – a broken heart), he shot himself in 1965. It was a sad blow to the world of motoring.

On the pit counter at Monza – Vittorio Jano.

twin-rotor supercharger. In 1924, its maximum speed was said to be 140mph (225kph).

It was the P2, more than any other car, which gave Alfa-Romeo its first true run of racing wins, and so it can be said that it was this car upon which the great reputation of Portello's sporting successes was built. Antonio Ascari won the P2's first major race, at Cremona in 1924. Then Giuseppe Campari won the Grand Prix d'Europe at Lyons in August that year, whilst Louis Wagner came fourth in the same race. Then came the first of many Alfa-Romeo runaway victories with the Italian Grand Prix in September 1924, when P2s took the first four places. In 1925, Ascari won the Grand Prix d'Europe, whilst Count Brilli-Perri won the Italian Grand Prix. The run of success that year was marred by the death of Antonio Ascari whilst in the lead at the French Grand Prix, resulting in the immediate withdrawal of the team from the race.

The experience gained from the P2 led to

the development of Alfa-Romeo's first production light car, the 6C 1500, which was announced in 1927. Developed in two versions, the 6C 1500 Turismo was fitted with a single overhead camshaft engine, whilst the Sport, introduced in 1928, had an engine with twin overhead camshafts and was fitted with a supercharger which endowed it with a power output of 70bhp. Then, in 1929, came one of Alfa-Romeo's truly historic models, the 6C 1750. Surely, no one in the world can have heard of Alfa-Romeo and not the immortal 1750?

Like the 1500, the 1750 engine was built in two versions, a single overhead camshaft for the Turismo and twin overhead camshafts for the Gran Turismo and Sport models. Superchargers were fitted to the Gran Sport and Super Sport models, which followed after the initial introduction of the 1750. This was a highly successful range and Alfa-Romeo truly made its name as a sporting car maker on the reputation of the 6C 1750, which was used by many coachbuilders of the day to display their art. One 1750 engine was even developed as an aero engine, powering a Caproni Ca100.

JANO'S EIGHT-CYLINDER CARS

Back on the motor racing front, Alfas had won the 1929 Mille Miglia, the Ulster Tourist Trophy Race and the Targa Florio. The old 1925 P2 had been revived and updated for racing, three examples having been bought back by the factory and refurbished. But these were getting rather long in the tooth now, and a new range was needed, to maintain both Alfa-Romeo's racing successors and its commercial momentum. So Vittorio Jano returned to his drawing board, tasked with the objective of repeating the success of the 1750 on the track and in the showroom. The result of his endeavour was revealed to the world in 1931, in the form of

an eight-cylinder car, taking much of the P2's experience to produce a 2.3-litre car named the 8C 2300.

As with the 6C models, Jano repeated the options of single and twin cam cylinder heads to give variations on the basic theme. The bore and stroke of the engine were the same as those on the 1750, giving a displacement of 2,336cc and a certain level of component interchangeability. In supercharged form, the 8C was capable of 180bhp, which made a match for many a larger car in competition. The most significant demonstration of its competitive ability was at Le Mans in 1931, where Alfa-Romeo was determined to break Bentley's four-year run of success. And break it they did, with an equal four-year run of success, commencing with the Birkin/Howe win of 1931.

Success followed success and it seemed that Alfa Romeo could not lose. Tazio Nuvolari won the 1931 Italian Grand Prix in an 8C 2300 Monza, and 8C 2300 Monzas went on to win the 1932 Spanish Grand Prix, the Monaco Grand Prix and the 1933 Targa Florio. The 1750 was revived to racing use in 1931, by installing two engines in a chassis which became known as the Type A, aimed at an unlimited capacity Grand Prix formula. It was not especially successful, though Giuseppe Campari won the 1931 Coppa Acerbo ahead of the favourite, Louis Chiron.

Regardless of his position, in 1932 Jano produced what some consider to have been his finest achievement – the outstandingly successful Tipo B, or P3 as it came to be known. With a body design based on the Monza, the new car initially had a 2,654cc straight-eight twin overhead cam engine, with a four-speed gearbox driving a differential mounted immediately behind it, so that individual propeller-shafts could pass to each rear wheel, giving better handling characteristics. It wasn't long before the engine capacity was increased to 2,905cc, whilst the dry weight of the complete car was only 1,550lb (703kg).

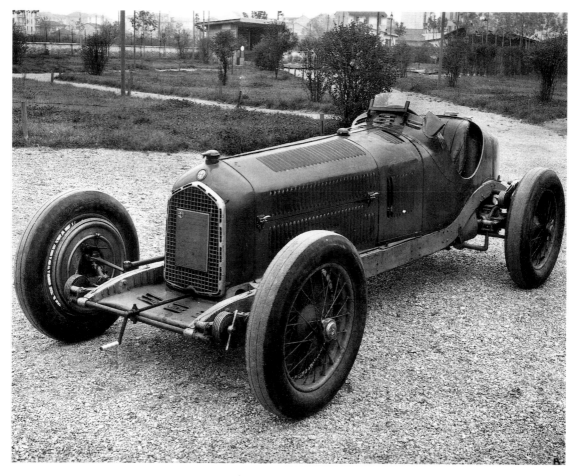

The Grand Prix Tipo B, or P3, built between 1932 and 1934.

The 1932 Italian Grand Prix, held on 23 June at Monza, saw the debut of these magnificent cars, two being among an entry of six Alfa Romeos from Scuderia Ferrari. They finished first and second, whilst a month later, the French Grand Prix witnessed an Alfa-Romeo first, second and third. Another Alfa 1-2-3 was the German Grand Prix, followed by a 1-2-3 in the Coppa Ciano and a 1-2 at the Coppa Acerbo. In the Monza Grand Prix, last of the year's major races, Rudolf Caracciola took the chequered flag.

This, then, was almost Vittorio Jano's last major contribution to the fortunes of Alfa Romeo, for 1933 saw the company plunged into a state of uncertainty as to its very future, leave alone what that future might hold. As the cash flow position revealed itself, support for racing was suspended, leaving Scuderia Ferrari the problem of whether to race entirely at its own cost, or whether not to race. Sadly, the latter decision was taken and Ferrari turned his attention to racing motorcycles with a team of British Nortons, whilst the Istituto di Liquidazione took possession of the assets of Alfa Romeo, pending the decision of the IRI. However, Enzo Ferrari did continue racing Alfa Romeos, as the factory refused in 1934 to sell cars to foreigners.

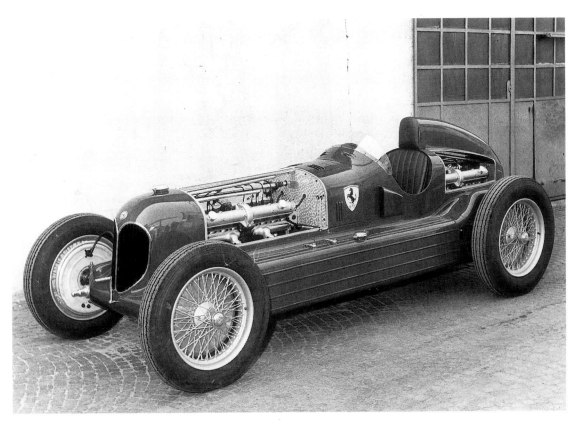

The Bimotore racing car – literally 'two engines' – from the Alfa Romeo Museum at Arese.

CHANGES OF DIRECTION

There wasn't much activity at Portello on the automotive front in 1933, though the 6C 1900 appeared as a production model, together with the 6C 2300, whilst the 1750 continued into 1934. During that year also, the racing P3 engines were bored out to 2,905cc and by 1935, the cars had reverse quarter-elliptic rear springs and Dubonnet independent front suspension. Then, in just four months, Scuderia Ferrari built a new twin-engined car for the 1935 Tripoli Grand Prix, using two P3 power units, one in front and one at the rear. This giant, aptly named 'Bimotore', came fourth and fifth at Tripoli, then second at the Avus Grand Prix in Berlin.

The Bimotore was not the answer to Alfa Romeo and Ferrari's racing problems, however, as it was heavy and complicated. So the 8C/35 Monoposto emerged from Vittorio Jano's drawing board, built and developed at Modena in Scuderia Ferrari's workshops. This new car had an all-streamlined body and was fitted with independent suspension front and rear. The first public appearance of the 8C was in the Italian Grand Prix, where Tazio Nuvolari drove a fierce race but suffered a piston failure two-thirds of the way through. So, whilst in second place, with victory in his sights, he did no more than take over René Dreyfus's Scuderia Ferrari 3.8-litre Monoposto. However, this car dropped a valve, so the best Nuvolari could achieve was second place.

A twelve-cylinder engine had been designed originally for this Monoposto Alfa Romeo, but it wasn't ready in time for the Italian Grand Prix in September 1935. Therefore, in 1936 a single car was taken to the Roosevelt Raceway, at Long Island in the United States of America, for the Vanderbilt Cup Race. Once again, Nuvolari was named as driver and gave a magnificent performance, winning the race with ease. But Mercédès-Benz and Auto Union were gaining ground and, to counteract their increasing successes, Alfa Romeo built a two-seat version of the 8C, to be called the 8c2900, to be fielded in sports car racing events. Three of these cars ran away with the 1936 Mille Miglia and so a few were built as sports cars for sale to the public.

The 6C 2300 had been performing well as a production car and so it was decided that it should share some of the limelight of its more illustrious single-seat racing siblings. As a consequence, an entry was made in the 1937 Mille Miglia, where the 6C 2300 Berlinetta Touring took fourth place overall and first in the Touring Car Class. Thus the 6C gained in popularity and some of the world's finest coachbuilders practicised their art on examples of this model to further enhance the reputation of Alfa Romeo.

THE LEGEND CONFIRMED

Given that only ten production cars are

The Mille Miglia 6c2300 Berlinetta of 1937.

Prototype and forerunner of a Grand Prix legend, this is the 1938 version of the Alfa Romeo Tipo 158 (the Alfetta racing voiturette). Here, it is seen being driven by Francesco Severi in the 1938 Grand Prix di Milan, where he finished second.

Also built in 1938, the full-blown Grand Prix car, the Tipo 316.

reputed to have left the Alfa Romeo factory in 1936, Ugo Gobbato called for a significant production increase for the coming years and so, some 270-odd were built in 1937 and a further 540 in 1938. The year 1938 was one of great moment for Alfa Romeo. This was the year in which, arguably, the greatest Grand Prix car in history made its debut – the Tipo 158, affectionately known as the 'Alfetta'. This new car was originally designed for voiturette racing (1.5 litre), as Grand Prix cars were still of much larger capacity. Designed largely by Gioacchino Colombo, the 158 was to raise Alfa Romeo's racing reputation to its highest pinnacle.

In 1938, Ugo Gobbato bought 80 per cent of the equity of Scuderia Ferrari, making Alfa Romeo its absolute master. This brought the racing activity back under factory control by the easiest and most decisive means, with Wifredo Ricart in ultimate management control. Alfa Corse was revived and Enzo Ferrari found himself under Ricart's supervision, a position he didn't like and

which was not destined to last. But, under these conditions, the Tipo 158 was conceived and built, along with the Types 308, 312 and 316, the latter three aimed at bringing back Grand Prix laurels to Portello, though none proved capable of the sustained high performance essential to winning. So Colombo beavered away on the 158 (which was certainly extensively influenced in its design by Enzo Ferrari), as well as the 3-litre Grand Prix cars.

The three 3-litre Grand Prix cars were eclipsed by the success of the 158, which, whilst designed by Gioacchino Colombo, had an engine that bore the hallmarks of Jano's designs of earlier years. On the bench, the 1,479cc engine had produced 180bhp at 6,500rpm with a single supercharger, though it was destined to produce much more before its withdrawal. In the Alfetta's first noteworthy outing, at the 1938 Coppa Ciano, 158s were first, second and fourth.

Alfa Romeo 158s were now to be seen in the first three places, sometimes in all three, regularly, on all the major racing circuits of Europe. The last race before the clouds of war gathered over motor racing for five years was the Tripoli Grand Prix of 1940, where the Alfetta's future was firmly set. Here, Giuseppe Farina won the race and set a new lap record in the process. But now, the racing circuits of Europe fell silent.

Italy was drawn into Hitler's war in June 1940 and the Alfa Romeo factory was directed to manufacturing the tools of war — trucks, buses, marine engines, aero engines and aircraft propellors. However, this did not deter the odd bit of development on racing cars when the opportunity arose. As a result, the Alfettas, which were kept in the Alfa Romeo workshops under the banking at the

Monza race track, along with the two 512s that were built, were the subject of quiet development until 1942.

In 1943, the Germans took control of northern Italy and in the process, they decided to take over Monza Park as a vehicle storage depot. Gioacchino Colombo realized he had to move quickly if he was to prevent his precious racing stable becoming German booty. He organized a safe haven for all seven Alfettas and the two 512s, along with the partly dismantled mobile workshop and a host of spare parts. That safe haven was a cheese factory in Melzo, not too far from Milan, where everything was taken from Monza and walled up until the end of hostilities. Hidden away, they remained at

335bhp from 1.5 litres, the exciting but unraced Tipo 512, finished in 1940, after war had begun.

The Tipo 512.

The Alfa Romeo 1900 Saloon.

Melzo until 1946, when a whole new motor racing era was to begin.

After the war, Alfa Romeo swept the Grand Prix scoreboard, developing the Tipo 158 to produce 425bhp by the end of its career, and winning just about every race in sight until they finally withdrew from Grand Prix racing in 1951. The charisma of this great run of success was used to the full and by 1950, a new small Alfa Romeo had arrived on the production scene, in the form of the 1900 Series. Not to be confused with the pre-war 6C 1900, the new car was powered by a four-cylinder twin overhead-cam engine and was first announced in four-door saloon form.

It was a solid, sensible car and was Alfa Romeo's first attempt at quantity production.

The 1900 was produced in Saloon and Coupe versions, as well as a military general-purpose ('Jeep' named 'La Matta') vehicle, and other versions by various coachbuilders who were attracted to it. These included Pininfarina, Boano, Carrozeria Touring and many others. Both Pininfarina and Touring produced drophead versions, Pininfarina's Cabriolet being announced in 1951 and a magnificent Spider built by Touring in 1954, revised as late as 1957. So the story of the Spider could now begin . . .

4 From Devastation to Duetto

THE RECONSTRUCTION

Roofless Alfa Romeos have been popular ever since Alfa Romeo gained any kind of popularity, but the Spider or 'Spyder' has its true origins in the development of the post World War II 1900 Series of cars. For this was the time when the company finally embarked on a programme of volume production and the 1900 Berlina (Saloon) was the first Alfa Romeo produced by volume techniques.

The Second World War had left Europe devastated, for what damage the Germans did not do in the period of Hitler's influence, the Allies almost certainly did in the name of securing victory. As a consequence, reconstruction was slow. Everything was in short supply, especially oil, so that when cars did finally come back into production, they were smaller than hitherto for two reasons. Firstly, the logic was that if a car were smaller, it would use less metal to manufacture, and secondly, if it were smaller, then it would use less fuel to propel it.

This simple logic influenced post-war thinking at Portello, just as in many other manufacturing centres. Whilst the badly damaged factory was being rebuilt, Alfa Romeo made anything it could; particularly, it manufactured a range of cooking stoves and window frames, just as a means of turning over money to enable it to pay its workers and to recover as a manufacturing unit. On the car front, there were stocks of components from the 6C 2500 Series produced before the war, and when the oppor-

Wartime factory damage at Portello.

tunity presented itself, design work was completed on a new two-door saloon. That car, the 'Freccia d'Oro' (the 'Golden Arrow'), was put into production in limited numbers.

In order to save royalties to coachbuilders, and in order to reduce the basic production costs of the car itself, the Freccia d'Oro body was designed in-house and the car produced entirely at Portello. However, it wasn't long before the famous names began beating a path to Alfa Romeo's door again and so chassis were released to such names as

*The 1948 production version of the 6c2500 'Freccia d'Oro' ('Golden Arrow')
Saloon.*

Pininfarina and Carrozeria Touring for them
to demonstrate their skills.

Because several coachbuilders produced
their own ideas of what the ideal sporting
Alfa Romeo drophead should look like –
bearing in mind how much closer everybody
was then to the great successes of the pre-war
days – the consequence was that an Alfa
Romeo 6C 2500 didn't really have much of an
identity. Everybody knew what the badge
looked like, what the likely performance of
an Alfa Romeo might be and that it was a
quality car.

It has been said of the 6C 2500 that you
could legitimately ask almost any enthusiast
for a description of what the car looked like
and receive a dozen, quite accurate answers.
Even so, it was with this model that the post-
war world of motoring sport in Milan was
revived to become a powerful force. Apart

from super-powerful cars like the 412,
carried over from pre-war days and rated as a
truly high performance car, the 6C 2500
came in Super Sports form, with a top power
rating of 110bhp at 4,800rpm, making it
quite a car for its day.

SATTA'S DREAM

It was in this period that Orazio Satta
Puliga, now Senior Project Engineer, decided
that Alfa Romeo needed to be able to produce
smaller cars in greater quantities, and at
lower unit costs. As a consequence, he had
his team concentrate their efforts on creating
a smaller car capable of being produced in
volume. That car was the four-cylinder engined 1900 Series. With a unitary construction, the design was a total departure for

Orazio Satta Puliga

'Dottore Satta', as he was universally known, was born in Turin in October 1910, the son of a doctor whose practice was in Piedmont. His father was a Sardinian and his mother half-Italian and half-German.

Orazio Satta Puliga was twenty-three when he graduated from Turin Polytechnic with a degree in mechanical engineering in 1933, the year Alfa Romeo went into public ownership via the IRI. He decided to remain at the Polytechnic to add to his qualifications, by securing a second degree, this time in aeronautical engineering. He was rated as a bright and methodical student with a brilliant flair for mathematics. His career track record confirms that early assessment.

Dr Satta joined Alfa Romeo under the patronage of Wifredo Ricart, and his first significant career break came with his appointment as Ricart's personal secretary, followed by taking charge of the Calculations Department in the Special Projects Department. When Ricart left Alfa Romeo in 1945, to return home to Spain, there was no doubt in the minds of the board of directors as to who should now be appointed Senior Project Engineer.

As he settled into his new post, Orazio Satta Puliga brought the highly successful post-war 1900 into being and re-established Alfa Romeo as a leading quality car maker, adding volume production on the way. He surrounded himself with a team of logical thinkers and doers. Among them were his old friend Giuseppe Busso, who left Ferrari to return to Portello; Franco Quaroni, who came from Pirelli and Rudolf Hruska, an Austrian, who came from Porsche. This was the team from which the ideas flowed to create two of Alfa Romeo's most successful cars – the Giulietta and the Alfasud. Imagine, then, the terrible shock to the automotive world in general and to Alfa Romeo in particular, when Dottore Satta died, on 24 March 1974, of an incurable brain disease.

Dr Orazio Satta Puliga with three of the famous products which came out of his department.

The 1951 4c1900 Pininfarina Cabriolet, the car which probably started the Spider story.

Alfa Romeo and, of course, it demanded a total change of technique for any coach-builder who might now be interested in placing his stamp on Alfa Romeos of the future.

The first successful demonstration, in Alfa Romeo terms, that the coachbuilders *had* adapted to unitary body construction came in the form of Pininfarina's 1951 1900 Cabriolet, followed by a government require-ment for a 'Torpedo Ministeriale', commis-sioned by the Italian Army in 1952. Soon after that, in 1954, came Touring's offering in drophead 1900s, a very sleek and attractive 1900 Cabriolet. For Alfa Romeo, the unitary-bodied drophead had arrived. Now, it was a matter of translating that into mass production, which would follow with the introduction of the Giulietta in 1954.

With over 19,200 cars built in the 1900 Series between 1951 and 1958, Alfa Romeo had entered the mass-production era, and though 2,400 cars per year average doesn't seem much like mass production today, it was a great leap forward in production

techniques of the time for the Milanese car maker. But Dr Satta and his team were not men to sit on their laurels, for no sooner had the 1900 been phased into production than they began work on the next Alfa Romeo model, which was to be the smallest ever.

The new car was released to an expectant world in 1954. It was the 1,290cc four-cylinder engined Giulietta Sprint Coupe, an exciting two-door car with a race-bred twin overhead camshaft power unit which had style, performance and economy, all in one package. It set the motoring press alight and was soon followed by the Giulietta Berlina, a four-door saloon styled along similar lines to the 1900 Berlina. Again, it was reckoned that the engine would be the strongest selling feature of the car – and it certainly was.

Alfa Romeo had done in Italy in the 1950s what Riley had done in England in the 1920s. They had created a car which they expected to be successful, but which had taken even them, the manufacturers, by storm with its success. For here was a car which used a small but highly efficient power plant, low on fuel consumption and, more importantly, low on vehicle licence cost, whilst having a performance little short of spectacular for its time. For example, the Giulietta Sprint Coupe was capable of 100mph (160kph) and yet could return as much as 40mpg (7l/100km).

THE SPYDER IS BORN

With this spectacular success, the company set about capitalizing on it as quickly as they could and by 1955, there was a Pininfarina-designed open sports car on the market, in the form of the Giulietta Spyder (or Spider). Like the 1900 Series before it, and its elder siblings, the Giulietta Sprint and Berlina models, the Spyder was built in a unitary construction, so had no separate chassis frame. The company which was to manufacture this body design – for it was decided early that Alfa Romeo did not have the space to set aside for production of this new model, other than final assembly – would have to make momentous changes to its construction facilities and techniques in order to be able to cope. That designer/manufacturer was to be none other than the house of Pininfarina.

Calculating that the name of such a world-

The Giulietta Spyder – first of a long line, this was Pininfarina at his best. Beautifully proportioned, this magnificent little car was good to look at from any angle.

Specification – Alfa Romeo Giulietta Spyder

Model *Giulietta Spyder*
Year 1955–62

Type 2-seat, 2-door sports roadster
Wheelbase 2,250mm
Track 1,292mm (F); 1,270mm (R)
Tyre sizes 155 × 15 all round
Brakes Drum on all four wheels
Suspension Helical coil springs all round, with unequal length transverse links and bar at front, upper triangular link and lower struts at rear
Engine 1,290cc twin ohc
No. of cylinders 4 in line
Bore/stroke 74mm × 75mm
Induction 1 downdraught twin-choke on Spider, 2 horizontal twin-choke on Spider Veloce
Ignition Coil and distributor
Power output 80bhp @ 6,300rpm (Spyder); 90bhp @ 6,500rpm (Spyder Veloce)
Transmission 4-speed gearbox in unit with engine, driving rear wheels
Gear ratios
With 10/41 Crown Wheel and Pinion 1st 13.358:1; 2nd 8.138:1; 3rd 5.564:1; 4th 4.555:1; reverse 14.81:1

Versions catalogued Giulietta Spyder, Giulietta Spyder Veloce

Like the Sprint Coupe, the Giulietta Spider was capable of around 100mph (160kph). It was of light weight and was soon to be offered with the Veloce engine as an option, which gave even better performance and dispatched the competition even more briskly. The engine was a light alloy unit with a bore and stroke of 74mm × 75mm, almost square, giving a power output from the beginning of the quite startling figure (for its day) of 80bhp in standard form, whilst in Veloce form, 100bhp was produced by the simple expedient of changing the single twin-choke downdraught carburettor for a pair of horizontal twin-chokes, as well as by improving the engine's breathing generally. The Spider only ever had a four-speed gearbox whilst produced as a Giulietta.

Talking of competition, there really wasn't

Specification – Alfa Romeo 2000 Series Spider

Model 2000 Spider
Year 1958–62

Type 2-seat, 2-door sports roadster
Wheelbase 2,500mm
Track 1,400mm (F); 1,370mm (R)
Tyre sizes 165 × 400 all round
Brakes Drum on all four wheels
Suspension Helical coil springs all round, with unequal length transverse links and anti-roll bar at front, upper triangular link and lower struts at rear
Engine 1,975cc twin ohc
No. of cylinders 4 in line
Bore/stroke 84.5mm × 88mm
Induction 2 horizontal twin-choke
Ignition Coil and distributor
Power output 115bhp @ 5,700rpm
Transmission 5-speed gearbox in unit with engine, driving rear wheels
Gear ratios 1st 15.566:1; 2nd 9.484:1; 3rd 6.483:1; 4th 4.777:1; 5th 4.080:1; reverse 15.537:1

Versions catalogued 2000 Spider

renowned coachbuilder as Pininfarina would promote sales, Satta committed Alfa Romeo to producing this new model in greater quantities than any open car his company had built before. In addition to that, he persuaded Pininfarina to undertake volume production of the body units, the first time a specialist had entered large-scale production of one of his designs. Over 27,000 Giulietta Spiders were produced before the model 'grew up' into the Giulia. Compared with just forty-two 1900 Cabriolets in 1953, that was a drastic change, which must have presented Pininfarina with colossal quality and production problems.

much around at that time, the German Porsche 356 Cabriolet, the British MGA and the equally British Triumph TR3 being just about it! The Porsche certainly had comparable performance with the Giulietta, though its engine was larger and there was still some curiosity about its rear-mounted air-cooled engine. Indeed, many people seemed to see it as a sports version of the VW 'Beetle', from which of course, it had its roots. The MGA, on the other hand, was a red-blooded sports car in the same idiom as the Giulietta and whilst it, too, had a slightly larger engine, the performance wasn't in the

(Opposite) As the Giulietta grew up, it became the Giulia Spider 1600.

same league. Even so, it had its own following, generated from MG's pre-war racing charisma.

So, Orazio Satta Puliga's gamble paid off, with the result that Alfa Romeo had it all their own way for quite a few years, allowing the Giulietta Spider to establish itself as Europe's leading small sports car – a title it justly deserved and, in the eyes of many *Alfisti*, has retained down the years. In fact,

Scaled up from the Giulietta, this is the 2600 Spider, which succeeded the four-cylinder engined 2000 in 1962, at the same time as the Giulia succeeded the Giulietta.

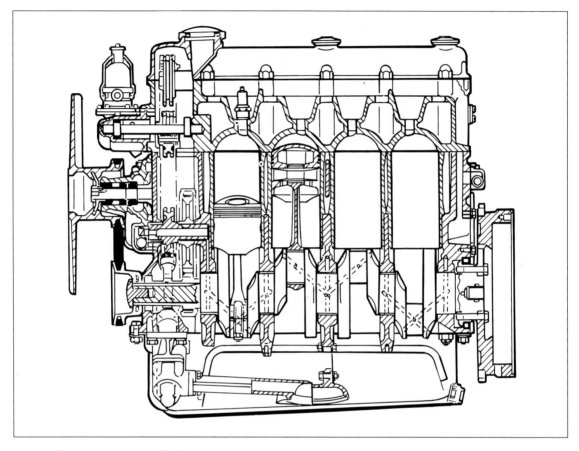

Longitudinal section of the Giulietta engine.

as the 1900 faded in 1958 to re-gestate as the 2000 Series for 1959, Dr Satta saw some point in talking to Pininfarina about repeating the success in that model.

It is interesting here to note that, like Riley twenty-five years before, the scaled-up version did not hit the market in the same way and so was not the same success story. However, it did progress (along with the whole 2000 Series) to become the 2600, with the new, much more powerful, 2600 six-cylinder engine. This engine was, again, a twin overhead cam unit in true Alfa Romeo tradition, with a bore of 83mm and a stroke of 79.6mm. Producing 145bhp in Spyder form, it is hardly surprising that this new,

larger car's performance was less than sparkling by comparison with its smaller relation. The 2600 Spyder did not continue in production for long, as it was seen to be competing directly in the face of Ferrari, which was bound to be the winner of that contest.

FROM GIULIETTA TO GIULIA

The whole range of Alfa Romeo models was revised and improved in 1962, with the result that the Giulietta name was dropped and all the cars in that range now became

SPECIFICATION: ALFA ROMEO GIULIA SPIDER

PERFORMANCE DATA
Top gear m.p.h. per 1,000 r.p.m.   16.9
Mean piston speed at max. power   3,335ft/min.
Engine revs. at mean max. speed   5,850 r.p.m.
B.h.p. per ton laden   86

ENGINE (front mounted, water cooled)
Cylinders   4-in-line
Bore   78mm (3.07in.)
Stroke   82mm (3.23in.)
Displacement   1,570c.c. (95.7 cu. in.)
Valve gear   Twin-overhead camshafts
Compression ratio   9.0-to-1
Carburettor   Solex 32PAIA5
Fuel pump   Mechanical diaphragm-type
Oil filter   Full-flow, renewable element, with by-pass
Max. power   92 b.h.p. (net) at 6,200 r.p.m.
Max. torque   108 lb. ft. at 3,700 r.p.m.

TRANSMISSION
Clutch   Single dry plate 8in. dia.
Gearbox   5-speed, all synchromesh, central control
Overall ratios   Top 4.05, Fourth 5.12, Third 6.94, Second 10.19, First 16.93, Reverse 15.43
Final drive   Hypoid bevel 5.12 to 1

CHASSIS
Construction   Integral, steel body

SUSPENSION
Front   Independent, wishbones and coil springs, telescopic dampers, anti-roll bar
Rear   Live axle, coil springs, trailing arms, telescopic dampers, A-bracket
Steering   Worm and roller
Wheel dia.   15.5in.

BRAKES
Type   Girling hydraulic, finned aluminium drums with leading-and-trailing shoes rear; three-leading shoe front, with discs optional
Dimensions   F, 10.65in. dia. disc. R, 10.5in. dia., 1.75in. wide shoes
Swept area   F, 232 sq. in., R, 116 sq. in. Total: 348 sq. in. (325 sq. in. per ton laden)

WHEELS
Type   Pressed steel disc, 4 studs. 4.5in. wide rim
Tyres   155 – 15in.

EQUIPMENT
Battery   12-volt 50-amp. hr.
Headlamps   40–45 watt
Reversing lamp   2 standard
Electric fuses   8
Screen wipers   Single speed, self-parking
Screen washer   Standard, pedal plunger
Interior heater   Standard, fresh air
Safety belts   Extra, anchorage provided
© Iliffe Transport Publications Ltd, 1964

Interior trim   P.V.C.
Floor covering   Pile carpets and rubber mats
Starting handle   No provision
Jack   Pillar type
Jacking points   Two each side
Other bodies   None

MAINTENANCE
Fuel tank   11.7 imp. gallons (no reserve)
Cooling system   13 pints (including heater)
Engine sump   11 pints SAE 40. Change oil every 2,500 miles: change filter element every 2,500 miles

Gearbox   3.2 pints SAE 90. Change oil every 7,500 miles
Final drive   2.5 pints SAE 90 EP. Change oil every 7,500 miles
Grease   16 points every 2,500 miles
Tyre pressures   F, 22.7; R, 24.1 p.s.i. (normal driving). F, 24.1; R, 25.6 p.s.i. (fast driving). F, 28.4; R, 29.8 p.s.i. (competition driving).

Scale: 0.3in to 1ft. Cushions uncompressed.

'Giulias'. The company also commissioned a new factory in that year, at Arese, about 6 miles north-west of Milan, as there was no further room for expansion at Portello. First of the new range of models, though, came out of Il Portello, including the Giulia Saloon, Spyder and Sprint models, as well as the new six-cylinder 2600 Series, which also consisted of a Saloon, Spider and Sprint.

The body styles of both the Giulia and 2600 Spiders remained virtually the same as they had in their previous guises as Giulietta and 2000, but now the Giulia was available with two engine options. Those buyers wanting the continuing economy of the 1,290cc engine could still have that version, but those wanting a more powerful and faster version could now buy the Giulia 1600 Spider, with its 1,570cc engine and five-speed gearbox.

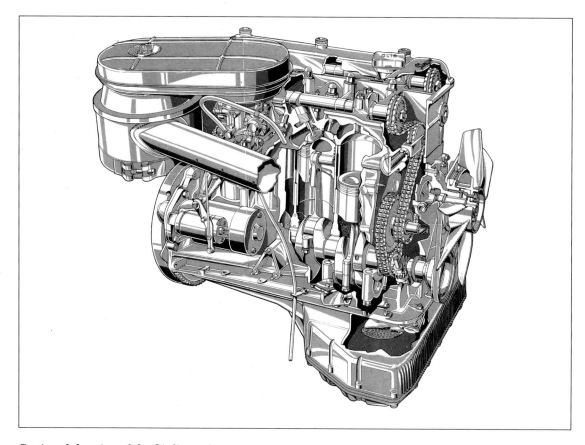

Sectioned drawing of the Giulia engine.

Very much the 'Giulietta Spider grown up', the Giulia 1600 could now boast some 92bhp in standard form or 112bhp in Veloce form (compared with 80bhp and 100bhp in the still-available 1300 form). The 1,570cc engine was a virtual enlargement of the smaller Giulietta unit, having a bore of 78mm and a stroke of 82mm, that slightly longer stroke aimed at giving a smoother torque curve. A superb little car had become an even better little car and, by 1966, was introduced with a re-designed body, still by Pininfarina, as the Alfa Romeo Duetto Spider.

The new Duetto took much from a Pininfarina design on the earlier 6C3000 chassis.

DUETTO AND COMPETITORS

Of course, by 1966, there was a very different range of sports cars on the market with which the Alfa Spider had to compete. Even so, there still wasn't much competition. The Porsche 356 had now gone, replaced by the Type 901, or the 911 as we know it today, the four-cylinder version of which, the 912, was a fixed-head coupe. The Speedster had been a huge success in the mid-1950s, but now it was gone and Porsche was out of the running in the open two-seater stakes.

Fiat on the other hand, now offered the 124 Spider, with a 1600 engine, which was quite

Specification – Alfa Romeo Giulia Spyder (1st Series)

Model Giulia Spider
Year 1962–65

Type 2-seat, 2-door sports roadster
Wheelbase 2,250mm
Track 1,292mm (F); 1,270mm (R)
Tyre sizes 155 × 15 all round
Brakes Drum on all four wheels initially, then disc front and drum rear
Suspension Helical coil springs all round, with unequal length transverse links and anti-roll bar front, upper triangular link and lower struts rear
Engine 1,570cc twin ohc
No. of cylinders 4 in line
Bore/stroke 78mm × 82mm
Induction 1 downdraught twin-choke
Ignition Coil and distributor
Power output 92bhp @ 6,200rpm (Spider); 112bhp @ 6,500rpm (Spider Veloce)
Transmission 5-speed gearbox in unit with engine, driving rear wheels
Gear ratios
With 8/41 Crown Wheel and Pinion 1st 16.933:1; 2nd 9.498:1; 3rd 6.944:1; 4th 5.125:1; 5th 4.054:1; reverse 15.426:1
With 9/41 Crown Wheel and Pinion 1st 15.051:1; 2nd 9.056:1; 3rd 6.127:1; 4th 4.555:1; 5th 3.603:1; reverse 13.712:1

Versions catalogued Giulietta 1600 Spyder, Giulia 1600 Spyder Veloce

Specification – Alfa Romeo 2600 Series Spyder

Model 2600 Spyder
Year 1962–65

Type 2-seat, 2-door roadster
Wheelbase 2,500mm
Track 1,400mm (F); 1,370mm (R)
Tyre sizes 165 × 400 all round
Brakes Disc front and rear
Suspension Helical coil springs all round, with unequal length transverse links and roll bar at front, upper triangular link and lower struts at rear
Engine 2,584cc twin ohc
No. of cylinders 6 in line
Bore/stroke 83mm × 79.6mm
Induction 3 horizontal twin-choke
Ignition Coil and distributor
Power output 145bhp @ 5,900rpm
Transmission 5-speed gearbox in unit with engine, driving rear wheels
Gear ratios 1st 15.768:1; 2nd 9.498:1; 3rd 6.944:1; 4th 5.125:1; 5th 3.779:1; reverse 14.381:1

Versions catalogued 2600 Spyder

lively, though not generally considered a 'real' sports car, whilst Lancia was concentrating on closed cars. In Britain, the MGB had now replaced the MGA, though again, its performance came nowhere near the Giulia Spider. The Morgan Plus Four was almost comparable in performance, but not in style or comfort, whilst such cars as the Reliant Sabre were seen as a bit of a joke.

One British car which was not a joke, and was a direct competitor with the Alfa Duetto, was the Lotus Elan. This was a car built in the same sporting character as the Duetto,

though with a few notable differences. The Lotus had a glassfibre body which was viewed with some suspicion in view of the problems owners had endured with the earlier Elite Coupe. In fairness, however, the lessons of fibreglass had been learned well by many in the intervening few years. The Elan was powered by a twin overhead cam version of the Ford 1600E engine and, despite only a four-speed gearbox, this little car was much quicker in a straight line. However, the Lotus had a separate following, largely because many people didn't understand or trust glassfibre bodywork then, so the Lotus didn't much dent the Alfa Romeo's market.

Further upmarket, the 2600 Spyder faced the might of Ferrari and Maserati, as well as competition from the Mercédès-Benz 230SL Series and the Austin-Healey 3000 – a big

Specification – Alfa Romeo 1600 Spider Duetto

Model 1600 Spider Duetto
Year 1966–67

Type 2-seat sports roadster
Wheelbase 2,250mm
Track 1,310mm (F); 1,270mm (R)
Tyre sizes 155 × 15 all round
Brakes Disc on all four wheels
Suspension Helical coil springs all round, with unequal length transverse links and anti-roll bar front, upper triangular link and lower struts rear
Engine 1,570cc twin ohc
No. of cylinders 4 in line
Bore/stroke 78mm × 82mm
Induction 2 horizontal twin-choke
Ignition Coil and distributor
Power output 109bhp @ 6,000rpm
Transmission 5-speed gearbox in unit with engine, driving rear wheels
Gear ratios *With 8/41 crown wheel and pinion* 1st 16.91:1; 2nd 10.199:1; 3rd 6.919:1; 4th 5.125:1; 5th 4.048:1; reverse 15.426:1

Versions catalogued 1600 Spider Duetto

The sum total of the market place in the late 1960s and the 1970s didn't add up to much in the world of sports cars, with the result that Alfa Romeo was able to advance its position with the various versions of the Spider without too much resistance. The late 1960s saw the Austin-Healey Sprite and MG Midget – a badge-engineered pair of 1,300cc open two-seaters with the same single cam pushrod-operated overhead valve engine that endowed them with a maximum speed in the lower nineties. The Triumph Spitfire was in the same league, but its pushrod-valved engine did little to help it compete, whilst Triumph's GT6 and Austin-Healey's 3000 were in a different market.

The Triumph TR4 was a gutsy sports car with a large-car feel to it. However, even with its 2-litre engine, it was no real match for the Alfa Spider where it mattered, in performance or handling, nor for that matter in its styling, looking a bit like a brick on wheels. The Vignale-bodied Lancia Flavia was an interesting comparison, with its front-wheel drive and 1,800cc flat-four engine, but it didn't dent Alfa Romeo's market much either.

In 1967, Alfa Romeo came up with an enlarged engine in the Giulia Series of cars, it being expanded to 1,750cc. So the Duetto name was officially dropped and the Spider was to grow up in the process.

brute of a sports car in the true British tradition – and several odd-ball specialist-built sports cars which never reached volume production, so didn't pose a threat.

The Giulietta and Giulia Spyders and Their Adversaries

Car and Model	Engine Type and Size	Gearbox	Max. Speed		Consumption		GB Price
			mph	(kph)	mpg	l/100km	
Alfa Romeo Giulietta Spyder	1,290cc 4-cylinder twin ohc	4-speed	105	(170)	30–35	(9–8)	£1,300 (1956)
Morgan Plus Four	1,991cc 4-cylinder pushrod ohv	4-speed	100	(160)	24–28	(12–10)	£969 (1958)
Porsche 356 Super 90 Cabriolet	1,582cc air-cooled flat-4 pushrod ohv	4-speed	111	(178)	24–30	(12–9)	£2,091 (1962)
MGA 1500 Roadster	1,489cc 4-cylinder pushrod ohv	4-speed	92	(148)	24–28	(12–10)	£940 (1955)
MGA 1600 Twin Cam Roadster	1,622cc 4-cylinder twin ohc	4-speed	102	(164)	24–28	(12–10)	£1,200 (1958)
Triumph TR2/3 Roadster	1,991cc 4-cylinder pushrod ohv	4-speed	105	(170)	24–26	(12–11)	£1,137 (1955)
Austin-Healey Sprite Mark 1	1.098cc 4-cylinder pushrod ohv	4-speed	87	(140)	30–35	(9–8)	£641 (1960)
Alfa Romeo Giulia 1600 Spyder	1,570cc 4-cylinder twin ohc	5-speed	109	(175)	26–28	(11–10)	£1,840 (1966)
Fiat 124 Spyder	1,592cc 4-cylinder twin ohc	5-speed	104	(167)	24–30	(12–9)	£1,400 (1972)
Alfa Romeo Spider Duetto 1600	1,570cc 4-cylinder twin ohc	5-speed	109	(175)	26–28	(11–10)	£2,025 (1967)
Lotus Elan 1600 Roadster	1,558cc 4-cylinder twin ohc	5-speed	115	(185)	25–30	(11–9)	£1,830 (1968)

Giuseppe Busso

Giuseppe Busso was born in 1913 at Turin to a family of modest means. He obtained a diploma as a P.I. ('Perito Industriale'). Like the mighty Jano, Busso was never a university graduate, but for all that, he established himself firmly as a thoroughly competent development engineer.

After completing his compulsory military service, he joined Fiat in 1937, working in the aero engine calculations office. From there, he later moved to the motor vehicles and railways' experimental division. In January 1939, Busso left Fiat to join Alfa Romeo, where he immediately went to work as assistant to Ingegnere Orazio Satta Puliga, in the calculations office of the Special Products Division. Here, he worked on much of the racing car technology involved with the Alfa Romeo 158, the Alfetta.

Giuseppe Busso did a great deal of work in the field of supercharging and turbines under Wifredo Ricart until 1945. Then in 1946, he left Alfa Romeo to join Enzo Ferrari at Modena, where he worked under both Gioacchino Colombo and Giulio Lampredi. In 1948, Dr Satta contacted his old friend and asked him to return to Alfa Romeo, as he had the need of a development engineer of Busso's calibre. And so, the prodigal son returned.

Busso was especially closely involved in the development of the 4C 1900 Series and the Giulietta. He did much work on the later Alfa Six and on the fuel injection systems for the V-6 engine. One area in which he had much involvement over the years, and about which little has been said, was the Centro Documentazione Storica and the Alfa Romeo Museum. He was very much a collaborator with his friend and work-master, Orazio Satta Puliga, hiding prototypes away instead of destroying them, in the hope that one day, someone would see sense and set up a museum. Eventually, Dr Giuseppe Luraghi did just that and many products of Alfa Romeo re-emerged, previously thought lost forever.

DRIVING SPIDERS

Back in the 1950s, the Giulietta Spider was being exported to the United States for a selling price of just under $3,000. There are many Americans today who would just love to buy the same car today for that price! Road testers eulogized over it, describing its handling as impeccable. The road adhesion was defined as 'uncanny', with moderate understeer, very light self-centring action on the steering wheel and virtually no body roll. One road tester was so impressed with the car's braking (drums, remember) that he was moved to describe them as 'close to, if not absolutely, the best we have ever experienced'. That's praise indeed, but fitting.

A couple of years after the first American road test came another, this time of the Giulietta Spider Veloce, with the 90bhp engine. After relatively little mileage, this car's second gear decided not to synchro-

mesh, though it did not impair the general performance of the car, which was described in similarly glowing terms to the earlier test report. Bottom gear maximum speed was said to be 35mph (55kph), whilst second saw 59mph (95kph) and third gave 86mph (140kph), all at 7,500rpm, some 800 revs over the red line. The best top speed achieved on a single run was just over 107mph (172kph), which was a pretty good turn of speed for a 1,290cc engine, pulling a car weighing in at just under 18cwt (935kg). The price was up some $686 but, in the words of another American reviewer: 'A car has no business being so desirable'.

The American magazine *Road & Track* road tested the Giulia Spider 1600 in 1963, commenting that there was really nothing

(Overleaf) Then came the famous Spider Duetto 1600 which, like the Giulietta, was attractive from any angle.

The Spider 1750 in its early form was a Duetto with an enlarged engine.

As the 2000 arrived, so the Spider shape was made crisper, with a more cleanly defined line.

Here, the 1971 Spider shows off the Kamm tail, which gives a more practical luggage space.

exotic about this car, unless one considers that it was among the least expensive sports cars on the market then with an overhead cam engine. Starting inside, the seats were said to be firm and to provide good support. The hood was criticized because the weather-sealing flap was not sufficiently well designed to avoid getting caught in the door as it was closed with the hood erected. But on the road, this Alfa, just like its smaller-engined predecessors, was given a very positive 'thumbs up'. The Giulia's drum brakes were described as a bit old hat by now, but were credited with being able to stop the car from 80mph (130kph) every bit as well as any comparable car could be stopped on discs. (This is probably true of that time, though disc brake technology has made vast strides in the years since then.) All in all, *Road &*

Track said that the Alfa Giulia Spider . . . 'maintains a stability matched by few cars available to the public'. It also commented that the buyer is getting just a little more than he pays for in an Alfa.

Wherever the early Alfa Spiders have been road tested, they have met with general approval from the enthusiast press, though electrics have come in for criticism at times, as have minor details, like door and window handles, odd bits of trim and Italian chrome plating. But they have never, ever, been marked down for roadholding and general handling. And when the Spider's next generation was born, beginning with the Duetto of 1966, it inherited all the outstanding qualities of the Giulietta and Giulia before it, setting in motion the creation of yet another legend.

5 New Directions

THE FRONT-WHEEL DRIVE DEBATE

Front-wheel drive is no new concept, having been around since the 1920s, but the mechanics of making it reliable, efficient, pleasant to drive, and therefore acceptable to the market place took a very long time to achieve. In fact, the car which did most to make the concept acceptable was Sir Alec Issigonis's Mini, introduced by Austin and Morris in 1959. (Originally, the Austin version was called the Seven, after its famous forebear of the 1920s and the Morris was the Mini.)

Even before the British Motor Corporation began work on the Mini, Alfa Romeo was conducting serious research into the processes and benefits of front-wheel drive. The 1900 Series was beginning to become established by this time as a successful model – indeed, as Alfa Romeo's *most* successful as far as volume production was concerned – but there was the continuing and pressing need to advance and produce the design for the car which would replace today's model. Furthermore, Alfa Romeo knew that a car with a 1900 engine was not striking at the mass market.

The Giulietta was a positive project by 1952 and there was no turning back, but the mass market appealed to Dr Orazio Satta Puliga, where he was convinced that there was scope for an upmarket micro-car in the under-750cc category. So a project labelled 13-61 was launched that year to research the value of a potentially exciting small front-wheel drive vehicle which could be produced cheaply and in large numbers, whilst retaining something of the reputation of Alfa Romeo.

THE 13-61 – A CAR THAT NEARLY WAS

The 13-61 was to be a front-wheel-drive vehicle with, for its time, a number of quite advanced features. Much of the design work on this potential new model was to be the work of P.I. Giuseppe Busso, a very bright mathematician who had first joined Alfa Romeo in 1939, when engineering was under the influence of Wifredo Ricart, as assistant to Orazio Satta Puliga. As Dr Satta's career grew, so did P.I. Busso's and the 13-61 was to be a demonstration of his conceptual skills.

Among the 13-61's interesting features were:

● Rack and pinion steering in a time when cam and roller was the most common method in the industry.
● Inboard front brakes to reduce the unsprung weight on the front wheels.
● A transverse engine layout to maximize interior space, with a gearbox driving a centrally positioned differential to provide equal drive-shaft lengths.

It had all four seats within the wheelbase and its body line would have done Alfa Romeo credit ten years later.

The engine of this new small car was quite a departure from Portello's normal practice. It was a 600cc water-cooled twin-cylinder, almost certainly half the then-projected Giulietta, which by this time would have been past the design concept stage and into product development. Suspension of the 13-61 was by means of a transverse leaf at the front, connecting to double wishbones and shock absorbers, whilst the rear tubular

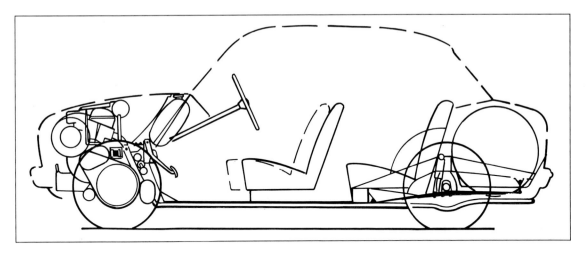

Layout drawing of the Tipo 13-61.

axle was supported by a pair of longitudinal semi-elliptic springs.

The target market for this diminutive four-seater was the top end of that in which the Fiat 500 was already established, aiming to be very economical to run, but of sufficient quality to lead its buyers on into other Alfa Romeo models as they moved up in car size. People thought about that kind of thing in those days and there is clear evidence to show that Alfa Romeo was very conscious of the need to attract its potential buyers as early as possible in their motoring lives and then groom them on to larger Alfa Romeos as they became better off. But the cost projections for the 13-61 proved it would be too expensive to produce at a competitive price, and it was shelved without even a prototype being built.

IF AT FIRST . . .

Not content to leave front-wheel drive to others, however, Alfa Romeo came up with another design for a slightly larger car in 1959. This was again a very stylish car for its time, but now was pointed at the Volkswagen/Fiat 1100/Renault Dauphine market sector, where the sales researchers perceived there was a market opportunity. Once more, the concept was to produce a car at the top end of the market, which would not only appeal to discerning young motorists, but which could be used to groom them into larger and better Alfa Romeo models later.

As with the 13-61, the new car, labelled Tipo 103, was to be a four-seat saloon, this time powered by an 896cc transversely positioned four-cylinder engine, with twin overhead camshafts in true Alfa Romeo tradition. The engine produced a creditable 52bhp at 5,500rpm and the prototype car, when performance tested, produced a standing quarter mile in 41.2 seconds. Not much by today's standards, perhaps, but not bad in its time. The four-speed gearbox was again connected to a centrally positioned differential, which once more assured equal-length driveshafts.

Only a single prototype of the Tipo 103 car was built, along with three additional engines: when the revised production cost projections were put forward, it was realized, in simple terms, that Alfa Romeo couldn't produce a car that good for so low a selling price as it would have needed to reach volume production. Even so, the company

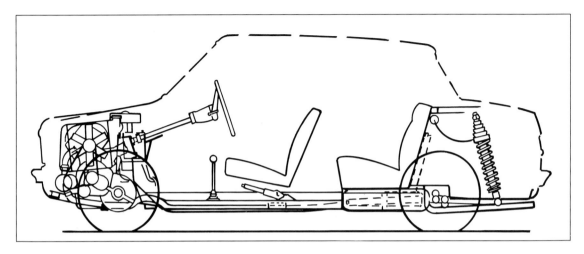

Layout of the Tipo 103.

The Tipo 103 Saloon, Alfa Romeo's first experiment in the metal with front-wheel drive.

persevered and it was to be 1962 before the Tipo 103 was finally abandoned. Meanwhile, a collaboration agreement with Renault had been reached, wherein the Dauphine was to be produced by Alfa Romeo under licence, and later the R4 as well. The need for an Alfa design in that market sector therefore was eliminated.

Because of the collaborative agreement, Renault showed a great deal of interest in the Tipo 103 and it would seem that serious thought was given to the use of the 896cc Alfa Romeo engine to power the later, rear-engined, Renault R8. Interesting, too, to observe that the RS bore more than a passing resemblance to the Alfa Romeo Tipo 103, when it appeared on the market not long

afterwards. Even as late as 1967, when the front-wheel-drive concept came back under the microscope at Arese, the Tipo 103 merited one last look before being finally abandoned for what was to become Alfa Romeo's most ambitious project yet, the Alfasud.

TO POMIGLIANO D'ARCO

Rudolf Hruska returned to Alfa Romeo, under the persuasion of Dr Giuseppe Luraghi, then President of the company, to develop a new small car in the character and market slot previously occupied by the Giulietta. Dr Luraghi gave Hruska the assurance that he would not only have complete authority over the design and development of the new car, but that he would have total freedom, within cost budgets, over the design, development and equipment of the factory where this new car was to be built. The car was, of course, the Alfasud and the factory was to be on the old site of Pomigliano d'Arco, which had been the home of Alfa Avio for many years.

Pomigliano d'Arco is near to Naples, in southern Italy, hence the origin of the name 'Alfasud' for the newly projected car. A site was acquired by Alfa Romeo there in the 1930s, mainly as the home of the aero engine division, known as Alfa Avio. An airfield adjoined the factory site, as numerous aircraft were fitted with Alfa Romeo engines and then tested from that location. Considerable aircraft movement took place from Pomigliano during World War II and afterwards, as the company continued to be strong in the aviation world for several years – indeed, it is strong today in the Italian engines industry, as part of Aeritalia.

When the collaboration agreement between Alfa Romeo and Renault was concluded, Pomigliano d'Arco was the site selected for that production work. Many

---

Specification – Alfa Romeo Tipo 103 Front-Wheel-Drive Saloon

Model Type 103 Saloon
Year 1960–61

Type 4-seat, 4-door saloon
Wheelbase 2,230mm
Track 1,270mm (F); 1,225mm (R)
Tyre sizes 135 × 13 all round
Brakes Disc on all four wheels
Suspension All-helical coil springs with unequal length transverse links and anti-roll bar front, oscillating arms at rear, with coil springs and integral shock absorbers
Engine 896cc twin ohc, transversely mounted
No. of cylinders 4 – transversely in line
Bore/stroke 66mm × 66.5mm
Induction Single downdraught monobloc carburettor
Ignition Coil and distributor
Power output 60bhp (SAE)
Transmission 4-speed transmission in unit with engine, front-wheel drive
Gear ratios 1st 13.86:1; 2nd 8.48:1; 3rd 5.61:1; 4th 4.21:1; reverse 18.49:1

Versions catalogued Tipo 103 Saloon, (only one built, with three engines)

The Renault R4 was also produced at Pomigliano d'Arco, as well as the Dauphine.

now well experienced in the concept of mass production, the Renault project gave them a great deal of useful experience in the small, low-cost car market sector. This was to prove invaluable in the market development for the Alfasud. After producing both the Dauphine (named 'Ondine' in Italy) and the Renault R4, the collaboration agreement was not renewed, as Alfa Romeo now had other ideas about Pomigliano d'Arco.

THE ALFASUD PROJECT

The year 1967 was the one in which Rudolf Hruska was charged with the task of setting up the new venture. The projected roll-out date for the first production cars was to be 1972. With his early experience being acquired at Stuttgart in the Porsche works, it is hardly surprising that Hruska should have explored the merits of a horizontally opposed four-cylinder engine for his new car, as this provided a number of advantages. Firstly, the engine could be positioned longitudinally and use an orthodox gearbox. The advantage of this was to avoid the torque-induced strain

buildings were modified for use, as a large part of the airfield was no longer in full use by 1959, so a minimum of new construction was required to accommodate the French car's manufacture. Whilst Alfa Romeo was

This cutaway shows well the structural design of the Alfasud body unit.

Rudolf Hruska

Often listed in Alfa Romeo documents as 'Rodolfo Hruska', with his first name Latinized, he was actually born Rudolf Hruska, in Vienna in 1915.

Rudolf Hruska graduated from the Vienna Engineering Institute in 1935 and joined Porsche in 1938. Then mainly a design studio, Porsche was responsible for the establishment of Volkswagen at Wolfsburg and Hruska was closely involved in the car's design development. In 1942, he was assigned to the Tiger main battle tank project, then after the war, he worked on the Porsche-designed Cisitalia supercharged Grand Prix car.

After a period in Italy, working on the Cisitalia project, Hruska joined Finmeccanica as a consulting engineer to Alfa Romeo, working on the 1900 Series. Alfa Romeo then appointed him Technical Manager in 1954, working on such diverse projects as truck body panels and the Giulietta car range. With the re-organization of 1959, following the appointment of Balduccio Bardocci as President, Hruska was made Works Manager at Portello. However, it seems that the new team didn't work too well, as Franco Quaroni went to Simca in France soon after the re-organization and Hruska followed him, working both for Simca and Fiat at the same time. Very soon after that, Dr Giuseppe Luraghi succeeded Bardocci as Alfa Romeo's President.

It was Luraghi who lured Hruska back to Alfa Romeo, with the promise of a total free hand in the creation of a new small car and the factory in which to build it. That car was to be aimed at replacing the original Giulietta in the hearts and minds of *Alfisti* worldwide. The car was the Alfasud. History tells us the rest. Rudolf Hruska left Pomigliano d'Arco in 1974 to return to Arese, where he assumed overall responsibility for design, research and development of all Alfa Romeo products.

The man behind the Alfasud was Rudolf Hruska.

Specification – Alfasud First Series 1200 Saloon

Model Alfasud
Year 1971–82

Type 4-seat and 4-door saloons
Wheelbase 2,455mm
Track 1,384mm(F); 1,351mm (R)
Tyre sizes 145/70SR × 13
Brakes Disc on all four wheels
Suspension McPherson strut coil spring with anti-roll bar in front, rigid axle, longitudinal tie-rods and coil springs at rear
Engine 1,186cc single ohc to each bank
No. of cylinders 4 – horizontally opposed
Bore/stroke 80mm × 59mm
Induction Single downdraught carburettor
Ignition Coil and distributor
Power output 63bhp @ 6,000rpm
Transmission 4-speed transmission in unit with engine, front-wheel drive
Gear ratios 1st 14.55:1; 2nd 7.97:1; 3rd 5.30:1; 4th 3.99:1; reverse 12.70:1
Versions catalogued Alfasud 2 and 4-door, Alfasud L 2 and 4-door, Alfasud SE 2 and 4-door, Alfasud N 2 and 4-door

on the car's front end structure, such as had been experienced in Britain on the Austin/Morris 1100 Series. The whole body unit could thus 'take the strain' and there would be no fierce movements of engine and gearbox under sharp acceleration or deceleration, eliminating the need for an engine torque damper.

Taking a leaf out of the much earlier 13-61's book, the Alfasud was to have inboard front brakes, aimed, as in the earlier design, at reducing unsprung weight on the front wheels. The Alfasud was a classic example of its chief designer having looked at the market place before putting pencil to drawing board. It was to be a lightweight five-seat four-door saloon car with front-wheel drive and handling characteristics which would enable it to carry the Alfa Romeo badge with pride. And that is exactly what Hruska produced.

The original engine was of 1,186cc, with a bore and stroke of 80mm × 59mm and a power output of 63bhp at 6,000rpm. For the first time ever in Alfa Romeo's history, a notched-tooth belt was used to connect the camshafts, one per bank, to the crankshaft. The valve gear itself was highly ingenious, with a bucket tappet sitting over each valve and a hardened steel set-screw in the centre of the tappet, acting as the direct contact face to the valve stem. There were two cams per valve, matched in profile, each operating on the surface of the tappet to either side of the set-screw. There was a hole right through the camshaft itself to facilitate adjustment of the valve, whilst the set-screw had a self-tensioning insert which eliminated the need for any kind of lock-screw or locking tabs.

The gearbox for the Alfasud was fairly orthodox, in line four-speed unit (with the space for the fifth gear designed in from the beginning, which wasn't long in coming), but with the differential positioned between it

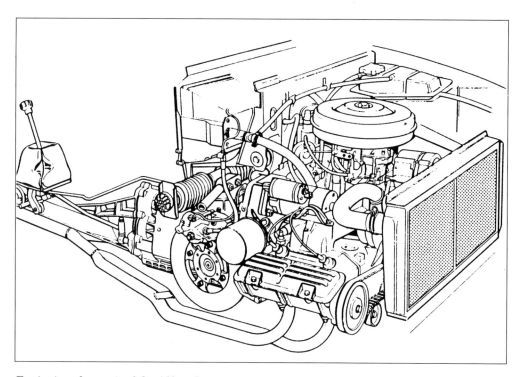

Engine/gearbox unit of the Alfasud.

This is the original Alfasud flat-four engine. Note the two cam lobes per valve.

and the engine. This gave two distinct advantages:

1. The weight of the engine in front of the driveline was counter-balanced in some degree by the weight of the gearbox behind the driveline.

2. The overhang forward of the car's front wheels was no more than it would have been on a car with a longitudinally positioned engine.

Styling of the Alfasud was entrusted to Giorgetto Giugiaro of Ital-Design, who took every advantage of the mechanical characteristics of Hruska's work. The front suspension, consisting of a MacPherson strut connecting to a wide spread bottom wishbone, facilitated a low front end and provided for good aerodynamic penetration, without inhibiting access for maintenance and repair. The interior was capable of being made spacious due to the minimal intrusion of suspension components at the rear, and it could be considered as a full four-door four/five-seat saloon. Because the rear suspension consisted of a fabricated beam axle, supported by coil springs and shock absorbers in the vertical plane, with trailing Watts linkage and a long Panhard rod in the horizontal plane, the luggage space was quite generous for so small a car.

Among the early proposals from Giugiaro were a longer rear end, which made the car too long for Hruska's intentions, and a more

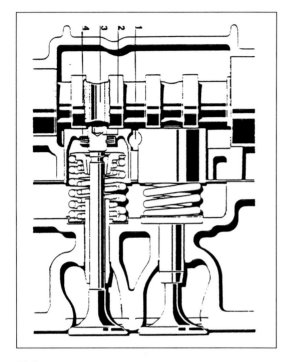

Valve gear.

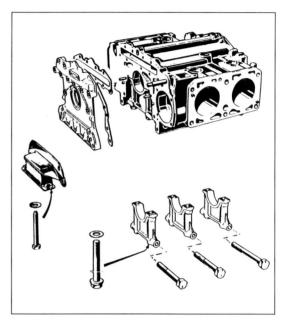

Cylinder block.

rounded front end than went into production, which was vetoed to the advantage of press tooling. However, the longer tail, with its recessed rear panel, appeared later on the Lancia Beta HPE and was accepted for that design, though none of Ital Design's present-ations were too far removed from the production version which appeared to the general public right on schedule in 1972.

Returning for a moment to the engine, one might have expected the cylinder block of a liquid-cooled flat-four to have been cast in alloy, especially for an Alfa Romeo engine. But that was not the case. Hruska's team decided that it was better to use cast iron, cost being a major factor, though the elimin-ation of the labour element in installing cylinder liners was another important point. This second factor wasn't just a matter of labour cost, but one of labour skill. It was expected that the work-force of Pomigliano d'Arco would be mostly workers with minimal motor industry experience, aided by the smallest element of skilled workers transferred from Arese in the training and supervisory role.

The Pomigliano factory, built as it was on the edge of the old airfield, allowed the construction of a test track adjacent to it, so the earliest driving tests of prototypes were able to be conducted well away from the prying eyes of the press. For cold weather testing, the prototypes were taken to Scandinavia, where their performance was found to be thoroughly pleasing to the management board of Alfa Romeo in Milan. Exhaustive testing produced a car capable of almost 100mph (160kph). (Some test cars actually achieved that magic figure, both at Pomigliano and at Balocco.)

THE DREAM COMES TRUE

First prototypes of the Alfasud were actually

The prototype Alfasud Saloon on winter trials in Sweden.

The first definitive production Alfasud.

built at Arese, as were the cars released to the press and industry for evaluation. Public launch date was November 1971, at the Turin Motor Show, and the new car received a rapturous welcome. It was a delightful shock when compared with other small cars of the time and the press wrote volumes of good material about it. Then the pilot production batch of 200 cars passed through Pomigliano d'Arco, on schedule, in June 1972. These were the first cars available for release to dealers who, like the press, gave the Alfasud a warm welcome.

As the car found its way into the hands of the driving public, criticisms began to filter back to Alfa Romeo. With only 16.5mph (26.5kph) per 1,000rpm and a four-speed gearbox, it was felt that the road performance fell rather short of Alfa Romeo's traditional standards. Some even said that the badge was a sign that it wasn't a real Alfa, as the word 'Milano' had been removed. Even so, the roadholding and braking were found to be excellent and the driving position was thought to be the most adaptable Alfa Romeo had ever produced, as tall drivers *and* short ones could make the car fit them with comfort. The plastic trim found itself the subject of comment too, though the reclining front seats were highly praised.

The Alfasud had an attractive rear aspect, too, this being the two-door 1.3TI Saloon.

Specification – Alfasud TI Saloons

Model Alfasud TI
Year 1973–84

Type 4-seat, 2-door saloon and 3-door hatchback
Wheelbase 2,485mm/Srs 3 = 2,455mm
Track 1,384/1,351mm/Srs 3 = 1392/1359
Tyre sizes 145SR × 13 early models – 165/70SR × 13 Series 3
Brakes Disc on all four wheels
Suspension McPherson strut coil spring with anti-roll bar in front, rigid axle, longitudinal tie-rods and coil springs at rear
Engines 1,186cc/1,286cc/1,490cc single ohc to each bank
No. of cylinders 4 – horizontally opposed
Bore/stroke 1.2: 80mm × 59mm; 1.3: 80mm × 67.2mm; 1.5: 84mm × 67.2mm
Induction Single downdraught carburettor
Ignition Coil and distributor
Power output 68bhp (1.2); 86bhp (1.3); 95bhp (1.5); 105bhp (GCTI) @ 6,000rpm
Transmission 5-speed transmission in unit with engine, front-wheel drive
Gear ratios 1st 14.59:1; 2nd 8.47:1; 3rd 5.88:1; 4th 4.60:1; 5th 3.82:1; reverse 12.70:1

Versions catalogued Alfasud TI 1.2, Alfasud TI 1.3, Alfasud TI 1.5, Alfasud TI Green Cloverleaf, Alfasud TI X 1.5

Work-force training began in earnest well over a year before the first metal passed down the production line at Pomigliano d'Arco. Some 7,000 people were recruited in the locality and transferred to Arese for intensive training in all skills essential to the mass production of cars. Many received training with Alfa Romeo sub-contractors, both in Italy and overseas. The training costs alone amounted to millions in any currency other than Lire. But it was all planned to be worth it, for here was the new successor to the Giulietta, which would be produced in far greater numbers than Alfa Romeo had hitherto even dreamed about. Over 21,000 cars were built in the first year of production alone and taking account of the fact that the Alfasud didn't start production until June, combined with the newly trained work-force having to settle in, that was a pretty fine record of achievement.

THE ALFASUD AT LARGE

Notwithstanding the opening production record, the early Alfasuds ran into a series of quality and reliability problems. On the quality front, there were such things as trim falling out of place. There were some criticisms about the quality of chrome plating and some owners found quite early that the hinges to the luggage compartment could easily be broken. Whether this last feature was entirely one of some faulty castings, or whether it was a design fault which allowed incautious users to break the hinges if they threw open the bootlid is open to question. It was, perhaps, a bit of both.

On the reliability front, there were experiences of carburettor flatspots at certain engine speeds, which translated themselves into near-accident situations when drivers found they had no power in such situations as pulling away. on crossroads in busy traffic. The wide ratios between gears on the early four-speed version meant that many an enthusiastic young blood would over-rev the engine between second and third, where the maximum road speeds were 49mph and 74mph (79kph and 119kph).

And then, there were the body problems. Many of the early cars showed a remarkably rapid tendency to decay through rust, which didn't help the reputation of the product any. Some people credit that to the use of Russian

The interior view shows how roomy the Alfasud was and how accessible.

steel, others to the application of quality control, rather than to the stated objectives of quality control. But the other feature which seemed to give problems in the early models was body rigidity, which was improved by a series of modifications, but limited the potential development of the design into Spider or Station Wagon versions.

Much of the rest of the quality problem lay with a labour force which was of questionable commitment. For example, whilst the production level for the first six months was pretty good, it quickly deteriorated, so that the planned rise was about half what it should have been – some

78,000-odd cars leaving Pomigliano d'Arco against a target of 175,000. Absenteeism was one of the contributory factors, with 57 per cent being reported at one point, but the true cause of the problem, seen with the 20:20 vision of hindsight, was that the ratio of experienced skilled workers and supervisors to newly trained workers was too low for the situation. Attitudes to work were different in the south. Levels of ambition were different, with a lower expectation of success or achievement. The consequence of that was poor labour relations, which translated themselves into strikes. But Alfa Romeo took courage and battled through to continue and develop the Alfasud range.

6 Development of the Alfasud Saloon Range

THE FAMILY LINE

There were three series of Alfasud – the first covering the longest period of time in the Saloon version's life – as well as two engine developments from the original 1,186cc version. Between the car's introduction and the launching of the Series 2 models, there were nine variations of Alfasud Saloon and the original two Sprints, the first of these being a 1300 and the second heralding the arrival of the 1,490cc Sprint 1.5 Coupe. These versions consisted of the original Alfasud Berlina (Saloon), the first TI with the 1,186cc engine; the Berlina SE; the Berlinas L and N; the Berlina 5M; and the first Sprint which, with the new two-door TI Saloon, heralded the arrival of the 1,286cc engine. Then came the two versions of the Berlina Super, with 1,186cc and 1,286cc options, accompanied by the 1.5 Sprint. The Giardinetta, or Station Wagon, was only available on the Italian home market.

Series 2 cars consisted of only six variants, these running between the years 1978 and 1980. First off the mark was another revision of the TI Saloon, which was now fitted with the modified 1.3 engine. This new engine saw the third increase in the stroke of the Alfasud's engine, the bore remaining a consistent 80mm up to this time, the new dimension being 67.2mm from the 64mm of the 1286 version, giving an engine displacement of 1,351cc. Following the introduction of the Sprint 1.5, which now had an 84mm × 67.2mm engine, there came another TI as an option to the 1350, this being fitted with the

---

Specification – Alfasud Second and Third Series Saloons

Model Alfasud 2nd/3rd Series
Year 1975–84

Type 4-seat, 2- and 4-door saloons, 3- and 5-door hatchbacks
Wheelbase 2,455mm
Track 1,384mm (F); 1,351mm (R) (Station Wagon) – 1,392mm (F); 1,359mm (R) (saloons and hatchbacks)
Tyre sizes 165/70SR × 13
Brakes Disc on all four wheels
Suspension McPherson strut coil spring with anti-roll bar in front, rigid axle, longitudinal tie-rods and coil springs at rear
Engines 1,186cc; 1,350cc; 1,490cc single ohc
No. of cylinders 4 – horizontally opposed
Bore/stroke 80mm × 59mm (1.2); 80mm × 67.2mm (1300); 84mm × 67.2mm (1500)
Induction Single downdraught carburettor on 2nd series – 1 twin-choke downdraught on 3rd series
Ignition Coil and distributor
Power output 63bhp (1200); 79bhp (1300) @ 6,000rpm; 95bhp @ 5,800rpm (1500)
Transmission 5-speed transmission in unit with engine, front-wheel drive
Gear ratios 1st 14.59:1; 2nd 8.47:1; 3rd 5.88:1; 4th 4.60:1; 5th 3.82:1; reverse 12.70:1
Versions catalogued Alfasud 5M 4-door 1200, 1300, 1500, Alfasud Station Wagon 1.2 (Giardinetta), Alfasud 1300 Super, Alfasud Super 1.3, Alfasud Super Gold Cloverleaf 1.5, Alfasud Valentino, Alfasud 5M 3rd Series 1.2, Alfasud 5M 3rd Series 1.3, Alfasud 5M 3rd Series 1.5

ALFASUD (1,186 c.c.)

ACCELERATION

SPEED MPH TRUE INDICATED	TIME IN SECS
30	4.6
33	
40	7.5
43	
50	10.4
53	
60	15.1
63	
70	21.7
73	
80	32.4
84	
90	—
94	

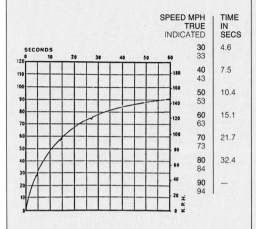

GEAR RATIOS AND TIME IN SEC

mph	Top (3.97)	3rd (5.31)	2nd (7.98)
10-30	—	13.4	6.6
20-40	17.0	10.7	5.9
30-50	15.2	9.9	6.0
40-50	16.1	10.2	—
50-70	19.5	11.9	—
60-80	26.4	17.3	—

Standing ¼-mile
20.3 sec 68 mph

Standing Kilometre
37.7 sec 83 mph
Test distance
1,008 miles
Mileage recorder
1.3
per cent over-reading

PERFORMANCE

MAXIMUM SPEEDS

Gear	mph	kph	rpm
Top (mean)	92	148	5,600
(best)	94	151	5,750
3rd	80	129	6,500
2nd	59	95	7,250
1st	32	52	7,250

BRAKES

FADE
(from 70 mph in neutral)
Pedal load for 0.5g stops in lb

1	25-30-25	6	30
2	25-30-25	7	30
3	30-35	8	30
4	30	9	30-37
5	30	10	30-37

RESPONSE (from 30 mph in neutral)

Load	g	Distance
20lb	0.30	100ft
40lb	0.68	44ft
60lb	0.84	36ft
80lb	0.98	30.7ft
Handbrake	0.32	94ft

Max. Gradient 1 in 3.

CLUTCH
Pedal 32lb and 5.2in.

COMPARISONS

MAXIMUM SPEED MPH
Ford Escort 1300 GT	(£1,082)	96
Citroen GS 1220 Club	(£1,347)	94
Alfasud	(£1,399)	92
Fiat 128 Rallye 1300	(£1,280)	88
Peugeot 204	(£1,316)	84

0-60 MPH, SEC
Ford Escort 1300 GT	12.4
Fiat 128 Rallye 1300	14.3
Citroen GS 1220 Club	14.9
Alfasud	15.1
Peugeot 204	17.4

STANDING ¼-MILE, SEC
Ford Escort 1300 GT	19.0
Fiat 128 Rallye 1300	19.6
Citroen GS 1220 Club	20.1
Alfasud	20.3
Peugeot 204	20.3

OVERALL MPG
Peugeot 204	28.2
Fiat 128 Rallye 1300	28.1
Alfasud	27.4
Ford Escort 1300 GT	25.4
Citroen GS 1220 Club	24.8

GEARING
(with 165/70-13in. tyres)
Top	16.4 mph per 1,000 rpm
3rd	12.3 mph per 1,000 rpm
2nd	8.1 mph per 1,000 rpm
1st	4.4 mph per 1,000 rpm

CONSUMPTION

FUEL (At constant speed – mpg)
30 mph	51.3
40 mph	46.5
50 mph	41.7
60 mph	36.4
70 mph	30.0
80 mph	25.3
90 mph	19.6

Typical mpg 30 (9.4 litres/100km)
Calculated (DIN) mpg 27.3
(10.3 litres/100km)
Overall mpg 27.4 (10.3 litres/100km)
Grade of fuel Premium, 4-star (min. 96RM)

OIL
Consumption (SAE 20/50) ......Negligible

TEST CONDITIONS:
Weather: Fine Wind: 0-9 mph.
Temperature: 21 deg. C. (70 deg. F).
Barometer: 29.65in.hg. Humidity: 70 percent
Surfaces: Dry concrete and asphalt.

WEIGHT:
Kerb Weight 16.9 cwt. (1.896lb-862kg).
(with oil, water and half full fuel tank).
Distribution, per cent F.63: R, 27.
Laden as tested: 20.5cwt (2,291lb-1,042kg).

TURNING CIRCLES:
Between kerbs L, 34 ft 4 in.; R, 31 ft 8 in.
Between walls L, 36 ft 4 in.; R, 33 ft 8 in.
Steering wheel turns, lock to lock 3.7.
Figures taken at 1,650 miles by our own
staff at the Motor Industry Research
Association proving ground at Nuneaton.

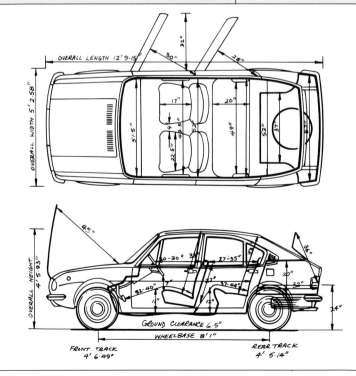

SPECIFICATION

FRONT ENGINE, FRONT-WHEEL DRIVE

ENGINE

Cylinders	4, horizonally-opposed
Main bearings	3
Cooling system	Water; pump, thermostat and electric fan
Bore	80mm (3.15in.)
Stroke	59mm (2.32in.)
Displacement	1,186 c.c. (72.4 cu.in.)
Valve gear	Single overhead camshaft per bank, cogged belt drive
Compression ratio	8.8-to-1. Min. octane rating: 96RM
Carburettors	Single Solex C32 DISA/21
Fuel pump	Mechanical
Oil filter	Full-flow, disposable can
Max. power	63 bhp (DIN) at 6,000 rpm
Max. torque	63 lb.ft. (DIN) at 3,500 rpm

TRANSMISSION

Clutch	Diaphragm spring, 7.08 in. dia., hydraulic operation
Gearbox	Four-speed, all-synchromesh
Gear ratios	Top 0.97
	Third 1.29
	Second 1.94
	First 3.54
	Reverse 3.09
Final drive	Hypoid bevel, 4.11 to 1

CHASSIS and BODY

Construction	Integral steel body and chassis

SUSPENSION

Front	Independent; MacPherson struts and coil springs, anti-roll bar, telescopic dampers
Rear	Dead beam axle; coil springs, Watts linkages, Panhard rod, telescopic dampers

STEERING

Type	Rack and pinion
Wheel dia.	15 in.

BRAKES

Make and type	ATE discs all round, divided hydraulics
Servo	Extra
Dimensions	F 10.15 in. dia.
	R 9.17 in. dia.

Swept area	F 268.2 sq. in., R 205.6 sq. in.
	Total 473.8 sq. in. (462 sq. in./ton laden)

WHEELS

Type	Pressed steel ventilated disc, 4-stud fixing, 5in. wide rim
Tyres—make	Various, Goodyear G800 Rib on test car
—type	Radial ply tubed
—size	165/70-13 in.

EQUIPMENT

Battery	12 Volt 36 Ah.
Alternator	35 amp
Headlamps	90/80 watt (total)
Reversing lamp	Standard
Electric fuses	8
Screen wipers	2-speed
Screen washer	Standard, manual plunger
Interior heater	Standard, air-blending control
Heated backlight	Extra
Safety belts	Extra
Interior trim	Cloth seats, pvc headlining
Floor covering	Rubber mats, carpet extra
Jack	Screw scissor type
Jacking points	2 under each sill
Windscreen	Laminated or toughened
Underbody protection	Bitumastic overall

MAINTENANCE

Fuel tank	11 Imp. gallons (50 litres)
Cooling system	12 pints (inc. heater)
Engine sump	7 pints (4 litres). SAE 20/50. Change oil every 5,000 miles. Change filter every 5,000 miles.
Gearbox and final drive	6 pints. SAE 90HD. Change every 20,000 miles
Grease	No points
Valve clearance	Inlet 0.014-0.016 in. (cold)
	Exhaust 0.018-0.020 in. (cold)
Contact breaker	0.014-0.018 in. gap: 62 ± 2 deg. dwell
Ignition timing	8 ± 1 deg. BTDC (static)
	22 ± 1 deg. BTDC (stroboscopic at 2,000 prm)
Spark plug	Type: Lodge 2HL. Gap: non adjustable
Compression pressure	Not available
Tyre pressures	F 25; R 20 psi (all conditions)
Max. payload	880lb (400kg)

	5,000 miles	10,000 miles
Service Interval		
Time Allowed (hours and mins)	1.15	2.30
Cost @ £3.30 per hour	£4.12	£8.25
Oil Change	£1.62	£1.62
Oil Filter	£1.63	£1.63
Breather Filter	—	—
Air Filter	—	£2.07
Contact Breaker Points	—	£1.53
Sparking Plugs	—	£3.30
Total Cost:	£7.37	£18.40

Routine Replacements:	Time hr min	Cost (labour)	Spares	TOTAL
Brake Pads/shoes — Front (set)	0.27	£1.49	£5.90	£7.39
Brake Pads/shoes — Rear (set)	0.24	£1.32	£5.81	£7.13
Exhaust System	0.30	£1.65	£38.32	£39.97
Clutch	3.54	£12.87	£28.84	£41.71
Dampers — Front (pair)	1.42	£5.61	£27.41	£33.02
Dampers — Rear (pair)	0.36	£1.98	£12.32	£14.30
Replace Drive Shaft	0.54	£2.97	£64.35	£67.32
Replace Generator (outright)	0.18	£0.99	*£104.31	£105.30
Replace Starter (outright)	0.24	£1.32	*£101.75	£103.07

*Exchange units will be available later for about £22

1490 engine. Late in 1978 came the Berlina Super 1.5, followed by the new 1.3 Super with the 1350 engine. Finally, to round off the Series 2 variants, the Sprint Veloce 1.5 arrived in 1979, whilst the last of the range was the Berlina TI S two-door Saloon, introduced in 1980.

Twenty-six variations of the Alfasud and Alfasud Sprint were produced in Series 3, which was launched at the beginning of 1980 and which drew to its close in 1984, with the demise of the Saloon version. However, that wasn't the last the world would see of a version of Alfasud, since the Sprint was re-titled 'Alfa Romeo Sprint' to continue in production until 1989. Essentially, this

First Series Alfasud 1.2 Normale at its announcement in 1972.

range of cars broke down into three basic groups:

1. The Saloons in 1350 and 1490 engined versions.
2. The Saloon TIs in 1350 and 1490 versions.

3. The Sprints in 1490 form up to the introduction of the even more enlarged engine version, the 87mm × 72mm (1,712cc) 1.7-litre of 1987–89, which were just preceded by the 1987 Sprint 1.5 Veloce. The Sprint Series of cars is covered in detail in Chapter 8.

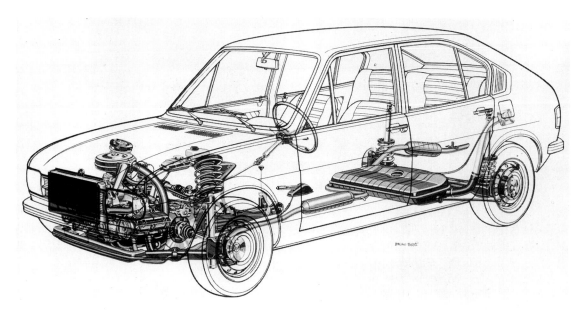

Looking through the Alfasud, we see why it is such a roomy car for its size.

EARLY IMPROVEMENTS

The Pomigliano d'Arco factory was dogged with problems throughout the period of Series 1 Alfasud production, but despite them, the single model available was soon joined by others. First on the scene was a new two-door TI version, which uprated the performance of the car by introducing the overdue five-speed gearbox, with better-spread ratios. This was coupled to an engine which gave five extra brake horsepower by the simple substitution of a twin-choke Weber carburettor to replace the old single Solex, whilst the engine's compression ratio was raised by two points, to 9:1.

Detail improvements which came with the TI included the use of four round headlights instead of the original rectangular pair, though the rectangular lamps remained with the Normale, or Standard, Saloon. Head restraints on the front seats were introduced with the TI, as well as carpets on the floor

instead of the rather Spartan rubber mats. The dashboard layout was revised to include a rev-counter and the always-useful parcel shelf. A more sporty steering wheel was introduced, with slots in the spokes, and by 1974, a heated rear window was available on both models, now joined by an SE (Special Equipment) version of the four-door, four-speed original car, with all the detail improvements described here.

THE GIARDINETTA

In 1975, there came a totally new version of the Alfasud, the Giardinetta, a three-door station wagon, which, it was felt, would broaden the market appeal of the car at home, in Italy. It was never offered for sale elsewhere in Europe, but does seem to have appeared in reasonable numbers on its home front, almost certainly a situation caused by the continuing pressing demand for the

Overhead rear-quarter view of the Giardinetta shows the clean lines and the full-height tailgate.

Alfasud Saloon, which was difficult to satisfy.

Body rigidity raised its head again with the Giardinetta, which had a heavy rear frame introduced into its design, to support the heavy tailgate and to prevent the tailgate from 'racking' in motion through torsional twist of the body. This one feature of the Giardinetta's design may well have been an influence over its non-appearance in other markets, though the suspicion was that it didn't go outside Italy simply because Alfa Romeo couldn't produce enough saloon Alfasuds to satisfy the market.

Rigidity was always a cause of some concern in the Alfasud – just as it had been in the original design concept of the Porsche 911 – and so the 'Sud' Saloon continued in production with a rear window and an orthodox luggage compartment at the rear. This went on for some years, and whilst it was the cause of criticism in 1972, it must be remembered that the original design layout for the car was set down in the mid-1960s, when hatchbacks were not yet popular. It would have meant a major re-design and, more importantly, greatly increased press

tooling costs, to make the change so late, though the Giardinetta, when it came, *did* have to replace the stiffness which was lost in extending the body length and providing an opening tailgate.

THE RANGE EXPANDS

Whatever the politics and economics of the Alfasud's variants, the little saloon was growing in popularity and so the company moved on and introduced many new versions. First in this long succession of variations and special editions was the Alfasud 'SE', already described. This was followed, in 1975, by the replacement of the two saloon models with two new variants, known as the 'N' ('Normale') and 'L' ('Lusso'), which in turn were supplemented by the 5M (*Cinque Marche*, or Five Speed). As its name implied, the 5M was fitted with the five-speed gearbox as standard, the first non-sporting Alfasud to forsake the original four-speed unit.

In its turn, the 5M was replaced by the Alfasud 1300 Super, though a version of the

The Alfasud 5M (Cinque Marche) with five-speed gearbox.

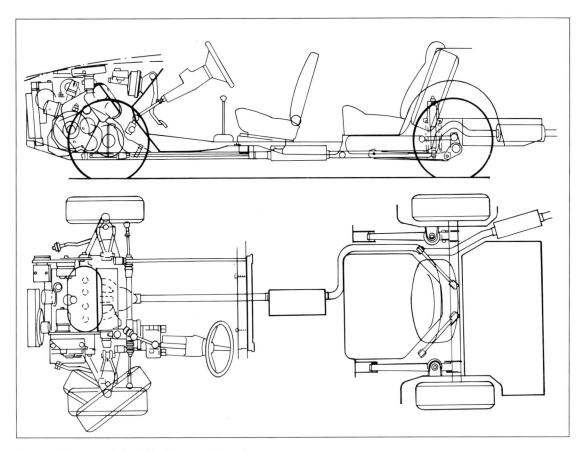

Layout drawing of the Alfa Romeo 152 project.

original 1.2 continued in production. This new engine was developed specifically for the Alfasud Sprint Coupe, with an increased stroke of 64mm, making the capacity 1,286cc, which passed on to the Saloon quite quickly and was also used to create a 1300 TI version. The Alfasud Sprint was introduced in 1976, as a latter-day Giulietta Sprint successor, though this is covered in greater detail elsewhere in this book. The one variant of the Alfasud which was planned, but never came into being, was a Spider version, again reputedly abandoned for fears that it did not have the requisite inherent body stiffness essential to an open car.

By 1978, the Sprint Coupe had been endowed with a 1500 engine, with a bore of 84mm and stroke of 67.2mm, to improve its performance and market potential against its competitors. The result was that its longer stroke was incorporated into a new 1300 engine, for production economy reasons mainly, so increasing the capacity of the existing 1300 engine to 1,351cc. This new engine came into the saloons and the 1,490cc '1.5' joined it as the 1.5 Super Saloon appeared.

ALFASUD OR 152?

At this point, we have to look back briefly, as

(Overleaf) The early Alfasud TI 1.3 Saloon.

the 1.5 Alfasud could easily never have come into existence. The niggling doubts in the minds of some of the design team were not yet dispelled and so a new concept of front-wheel-drive car went on to the drawing boards at Arese. This was the Tipo 152, which was devised as front-wheel drive, but was intended to utilize a developed version of the Giulia engine, positioned transversely – as were most front-wheel-drive designs throughout Europe at that time.

Lying at the root of the decision to explore this new design were the seemingly incessant problems of production at Pomigliano d'Arco. It almost seemed at that time that there would never be capacity production of the Alfasud, though it would have been impossible to produce it at Arese. However, there appears to have been a school of thought which subscribed to the idea that a front-wheel-drive car with Giulia mechanicals – in other words, a car powered by what was already being manufactured there – might succeed completely, where the Alfasud's success was so far qualified.

Two versions of the 152 were proposed, with 1,300cc and 1,600cc engines, designed to produce 105 and 120bhp respectively. The car was to have a wheelbase of 2,600mm, with interior accommodation near to that of the Alfetta Saloon. The smaller-engined version was to have a four-speed gearbox, whilst the 1600 would have had a five-speed. A very respectable 114mph (183kph) would have resulted for the 1600's top speed, whilst the 1300's maximum of 107mph (172kph) would have made it no slouch.

Suspension was to featured torsion bars at the front and longitudinal trailing arms at the rear, connected to a rigid axle and coil springs, much like the Alfasud in layout. Four disc brakes were included in the design to stop the car, whilst rack and pinion steering would have pointed it in the right direction. Had it been economic to produce, and had the engine of the Alfasud not been the success it was, this new car might well

---

Specification – Alfa Romeo Tipo 152 Front Wheel Drive Saloon

Model Type 152
Year 1974

Type 5-seat, 4-door saloon
Wheelbase 2,600mm
Track 1,370mm (F); 1,350mm (R)
Tyre sizes 185/70R × 13 all round
Brakes Disc on all four wheels
Suspension All-helical coil springs with unequal length transverse links and anti-roll bar front, triangular upper link and lower struts rear
Engines 1,360cc/1,623cc dohc, tranversely mounted
No. of cylinders 4 – transversely in line
Bore/stroke 1,360cc: 83mm × 75mm; 1,623cc: 78mm × 82mm
Induction 2 downdraught twin-choke
Ignition Coil and distributor
Power output 1,360cc: 105bhp @ 6,200rpm; 1,623cc: 120bhp @ 6,000rpm
Transmission 5-speed gearbox in unit with engine, front-wheel drive

Versions catalogued 152 1300 Saloon, 152 1600 Saloon

---

have taken the place of the Alfasud and been a worthy successor.

As the design exercise progressed for the Alfa Romeo Tipo 152, it became clear that the production costs for such a car would far exceed those of the Alfasud, even allowing for the fact that the Pomigliano d'Arco plant was not making its proper contribution to the company's overhead recoveries. However, the flat-four engine had gained much respect and was beginning to be accepted by even the most rearguard Alfa Romeo engineers as a viable power unit. It appears to have been as much this feature as any economic justification that finally won the day for the Alfasud. So the transverse engine in front-wheel-drive configuration had to wait a few more years before it was to succeed – and even then, not at the expense of the Boxer unit, which remains, in much-developed form, in production as you read this.

BACK TO POMIGLIANO D'ARCO

With the 152 now firmly set in history, the 1978 line-up of Alfasud Saloons consisted of the basic 1.2, the 1.3 Super, the 1.3 TI and the 1.5 Super. A year later came the 1.5 TI, as well as the various Sprint models which came along to supplement the product line. It was fast becoming a prolific range of cars and all successful, each in their own way.

The new decade was seen in by Alfa Romeo changing a number of details to improve the image of the Alfasud, without doing much to affect production costs. This was the Series 3 Alfasud, upon which bright metal parts, which had already moved from chrome to stainlesss steel, were replaced with matt black trim. The rear badge was no longer just 'Alfasud', but 'Alfa Romeo', with Alfasud added as a model name, rather than implying the marque name as had hitherto been the case. The bumpers became plastic and the radiator grille was improved, whilst black plastic side body trims reduced the risk of knocking off paint in car parks as

occupants opened the doors. The headlamp and tail-lamp designs were improved, too, whilst inside, dashboard and trim improvements all helped the intention of moving the image of the Alfasud further upmarket.

The most significant development for the Alfasud Saloon was to come in March 1981. From the earliest days of the car, press and public alike had asked why it was not available as a hatchback. Body rigidity was the unpublished clear answer and Alfa Romeo continued producing the car in its original body form for almost nine years. But then came a breakthrough, the 1981 Alfasud Hatchback. The bodyshell went back to the drawing board, certainly as a process of evolution, but possibly influenced by the need for press tool renovation and improvements, so the opportunity was seized to incorporate a hatchback rear door to replace the bootlid.

The new version received an unqualified welcome from all who had any interest to express in the Alfasud and it wasn't long before the hatchback was outselling the saloons. In customary Alfa Romeo tradition, the old model continued in production alongside the new for some time, though by the end of the year of the hatchback's introduction (1981), the two- and four-door saloons had disappeared from the product

The Alfasud Saloons and Their Adversaries							
Car and Model	Engine Type and Size	Gearbox	Max. Speed		Consumption		GB Price
			mph	(kph)	mpg	l/100km	
Alfasud Saloon 1.2	1,186cc flat-single ohc per bank	4-speed	102	(164)	28–36	(10–8)	£2,999 (1979)
Austin Allegro 1300	1,275cc 4-cylinder pushrod ohv	4-speed	85	(137)	29–36	(10–8)	£2,830 (1979)
Fiat Ritmo 1.3	1,301cc 4-cylinder single ohc	4-speed	98	(158)	28–36	(10–8)	£2,750 (1979)
Alfasud Saloon 1.3	1,351cc flat-4 single ohc per bank	5-speed	103	(166)	26–30	(11–9)	£3,271 (1979)
Colt Mirage 1.4	1,410cc 4-cylinder single ohc	4-speed	100	(160)	30–38	(9–7)	£2,400 (1979)
Chrysler Sunbeam 1.3	1,295cc 4-cylinder pushrod ohv	4-speed	83	(133)	28–35	(10–8)	£2,620 (1979)
Alfasud 1.5 Quadrifoglio Verde	1,490cc flat-4 single ohc per bank	5-speed	105	(170)	28–36	(10–8)	£5,325 (1982)
Lancia Delta Saloon	1,498cc 4-cylinder single ohc	5-speed	100	(160)	28–34	(10–8)	£4,995 (1982)
Talbot Horizon 1.5 GLS	1,442cc 4-cylinder pushrod ohv	5-speed	103	(166)	28–35	(10–8)	£4,981 (1982)
Volkswagen Golf GLS	1,457cc 4-cylinder single ohc	5-speed	101	(162)	28–38	(10–7)	£5,200+ (1982)
Alfasud 1.5TI	1,490cc flat-4 single ohc per bank	5-speed	108	(174)	28–32	(10–9)	£4,737 (1982)
Volkswagen Golf GTi	1,588cc 4-cylinder ohc	5-speed	117	(180)	28–35	(10–8)	£5,400+ (1982)

The Alfasud Super first had a 1.3 engine, as here.

line in favour of three- and five-door hatchbacks. This, then, was the final phase in the development of the Alfasud Saloon series of cars.

First of the new hatchback Alfasuds was the three-door TI 1.3, powered by the 1,351cc engine, accompanied by the 1.5, both introduced into the British market in February 1981. Just a month later came the lower-powered saloon versions in 1.3 and 1.5 forms although, as if to confirm that the old models were not yet dead, late in 1981 came revamped hatchbacks, accompanied by two-

Spats around the wheel arches and black trim identify the Series 2 TI from its predecessor.

Alfasud ti

This is the 1982/83 Alfasud 1.5SC Hatchback.

Last of its line, the 1983 Alfasud TI Green Cloverleaf 1.5 Saloon.

and four-door saloons, also in 1.3 and 1.5 versions. The TI Veloce 1.3 and 1.5 three-door hatchbacks completed the line-up for the 1981–82 Season.

At last, June 1982 saw the first five-door hatchbacks in the Alfasud range, with a line-up of four new models: the Berlina, or Saloon, 1.3 Five-Door, the Berlina SC 1.5 Five-Door and the Berlina Gold Cloverleaf Five-Door. This last version proved to be the fastest Alfasud Saloon produced, outside the TI versions, with a maximum speed of 106mph (170kph) against the three-door TIx's 108mph (174kph), claimed when it was announced in July 1982. Finally, in February 1983 came the last two new variants of the Alfasud Hatchback, the Berlina TI Green Cloverleaf, a 1.5 engined machine capable of 112mph (180kph), and the Berlina TI Veloce 1.3, with a mere 105mph (169kph) top speed.

The Alfasud had enjoyed a superb run for its money and, by the time its day came for replacement, it had become an excellent car, with a good service record. It had also generated a huge band of loyal enthusiasts, while body rust had been drastically reduced by careful metal treatments and selection of raw materials, as well as a bit of judicious improvement of water traps in the body pressings. Next in line of succession was to be the Arna, a short-lived inheritor of the Alfasud's mechanical components, which in turn was succeeded by the Alfa 33, borrower of another illustrious racing name. This last model was a car which was to keep the flat-four engine in production and, as we shall see later, justify its development into a power unit capable of more than twice the original power output of the initial 1,186cc engine of 1972.

ALFASUD SPECIAL EDITIONS

The early 1980s was a period when special

Specification – Alfa Romeo Arna Hatchbacks

Model Arna Series
Year 1983–86

Type 4-seat, 3- and 5-door hatchbacks
Wheelbase 2,415mm
Track 1,392mm (F); 1,402mm (R)
Tyre sizes 165/70SR × 13 (S/SL); 175/70SR × 13 (1.3 & 1.5TI)
Brakes Disc on all four wheels
Suspension McPherson strut coil spring with anti-roll bar in front, rigid axle with A-frame and coil springs at rear
Engines: 1,186cc/1,350cc/1,490cc sohc to each bank
No. of cylinders 4 – horizontally opposed
Bore/stroke 80mm × 59mm (1.2); 80mm × 67.2mm (1.3); 84mm × 67.2mm (1.5)
Induction Single downdraught carburettor on S/SL models – 2 twin-choke downdraught on TI models
Ignition Coil and distributor
Power output 63bhp @ 6,000rpm (1.2); 71bhp @ 5,800rpm (1.3SL); 86bhp (1.3TI) @ 5,800rpm; 95bhp @ 5,800rpm (1.5TI)
Transmission 5-speed transmission in unit with engine, front-wheel drive
Gear ratios 1st 14.55:1; 2nd 7.954:1; 3rd 5.381:1; 4th 3.985:1; 5th 3.201:1; reverse 11.993:1

Versions catalogued Arna 1.2L 3-door, Arna 1.2SL 5-door, Arna 1.3SL 5-door, Arna 1.3TI 3-door, Arna 1.5TI 3-door

---

editions were popular with the public and a very useful means of boosting otherwise flagging sales after the 1979 oil crisis. Alfa Romeo saw this as quickly as anyone else and was soon offering such editions as the 'Valentino' and later the 'Junior', the latter being an attempt to produce a lower priced Alfasud for the young driver about to acquire his or her first new car.

The Valentino was clearly aimed at the feminine market, the name alone seeking to

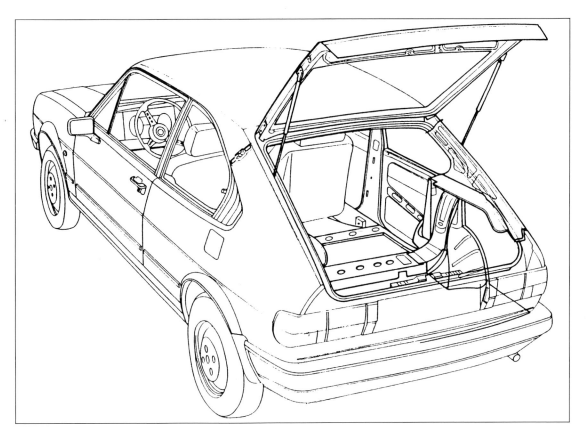

Alfasud Hatchback.

stir female Italian blood. Inside was velour trim, whilst outside, it was finished in metallic paint and had a side-stripe which extended up the rear quarter panel. This had the effect of reducing the height of the car to the untrained eye. The name 'Valentino' appeared in block capitals on the rear quarter panel to finish off the car. The Junior had the original 1200 engine, basic interior trim and a tricolour stripe down the side of the car, with the word 'Junior' on the tail.

There was also a more serious side to the production of special editions in Alfa Romeo's book and this was demonstrated by their research into vehicle safety and impact resistance, using the Alfasud Saloon from the inception of the Series 3 cars. Two such Alfasuds were developed for detailed

Valentino trim.

Here, you can see the distinctive rear trim of the Valentino Alfasud.

research and experimentation into energy saving and structural safety. One was aimed at developing cleaner, environment-friendly engines, combined with improved aerodynamic efficiency to conserve fuel, whilst the other was created to retain the integrity of the passenger compartment under a range of widely varying accident-impact conditions.

In November 1982, the 9th International Technical Conference on Vehicle Safety Experiments was held at Kyoto, in Japan. Here, Alfa Romeo revealed to the world's motor industry what *it* was doing about making a contribution to improving active and passive safety in passenger care. ESVAR (Energy Saving Vehicle Alfa Romeo) and SVAR (Synthesis Vehicle Alfa Romeo) demonstrated Alfa Romeo's commitment to environmental and fuel economy issues by minimizing fuel wastage and so atmospheric

pollution, as well as taking active safety measures in developing impact-resistant vehicle bodies, providing greater passenger safety.

ENERGY SAVING VEHICLE ALFA ROMEO (ESVAR)

The first stage in Alfa Romeo's development of an environment and passenger friendly car was energy saving. It was decided that the maximum energy could be saved by changing known factors first, such as reducing vehicle weight and improving the performance of the car's shape. So, various experiments were carried out in this direction, changing gear ratios, reducing rolling resistance, taking out weight and 'cleaning-up' the basic aerodynamics.

Weight and rolling resistance were the first two areas to be attacked, with the car's penetration through the air being next, for the extent of improvements achieved in these areas would dictate what were to be the final gear ratios capable of being used. Furthermore, all these tasks were undertaken with the clear understanding that every change made had to be capable of being translated into mass production.

Then came the engine's turn for attention. Clearly, you could choose almost any set of gear ratios you might think right for fuel efficiency, but without the engine performance to support it, the whole project would fail. So an electronic engine management system was created for Alfa Romeo, taking its specification from the company's stated objectives of increasing torque and power output by burning fuel more completely, so using less and giving a cleaner exhaust emission level. All features which directly affected the issue of environmental pollution.

The CEM system used microprocessors to control both fuel supply and ignition in the 1,490cc Alfasud Boxer engine. It therefore follows that fuel injection was to be the

Colour cutaway of the ESVAR/SVAR Alfasud.

The ESVAR engine showing fuel injection and CEM unit.

means of fuel supply, instead of carburettors. The fuel air mixture was regulated to produce what in modern parlance is called a 'lean-burn' characteristic, whilst the ignition timing was made more widely controllable and operating temperatures improved to achieve the end result. The compression ratio of the engine was also changed. Perhaps surprisingly, it was increased from 9.5:1 up to 10.2:1, and a cut-off system was introduced, to cut off fuel supply during the up-stroke of the piston.

Next came a step which has been tried many times down the years on larger engines, but never on such a small engine as a 1,500cc four-cylinder, and particularly not with a horizontally opposed engine. Here, two of the four cylinders were shut down by the CEM system under light load or when the engine was idling. Sensors in the induction ports related the angle of the throttle valve to the engine speed and state of ignition advance, and automatically cut out two cylinders under the right conditions, all aimed at improving the lean-burn nature of the engine.

The ultimate result of this engine development was a greatly improved torque output,

The ESVAR Alfasud in finished form. Note the aerodynamically 'clean' appearance, with front air dam and rear spoiler.

a power output equal to the original 1490 engine, but using a lower engine speed – 5,400rpm instead of 6,000rpm – to yield 95bhp.

The whole car's performance was also improved immensely, in terms of top speed and of acceleration from a standing start. Maximum speed of ESVAR was 115mph (185kph), against 108mph (174kph) for the TI Saloon, whilst the 0–60mph (0–100kph) time was improved to 9.8 seconds from 10.7, while the 1,000 metres standing start time was reduced by over 1¼ seconds. All this and using less fuel!

The lessons from the ESVAR experiment have been applied subsequently in the process of developing the quad-cam Boxer engine, which has phased valve timing, a comprehensive engine management system which controls fuel injection and ignition timing and leaner burn characteristics. It is this engine upon which much of Alfa Romeo's future engineering strategy is to depend and four-wheel drive will form part of that strategy, proving just how reliable and durable the Boxer engine has become.

SYNTHESIS VEHICLE ALFA ROMEO (SVAR)

The active safety aspect of Alfa Romeo's work resulted in the construction of a body with longitudinally placed, corrugated stiffening sections in the doors, which would help limit the yield of those panels on impact, so protecting better than hitherto the occupants of the car. Reinforcement to the front and rear structures were also a feature of the experiment, as well as a strengthened roof and re-designed bonnet panel, all aiming to make a much safer box in which people could travel. This was SVAR.

Whilst aerodynamics were researched in the ESVAR programme, aiming to reduce fuel consumption and maximize operating efficiency, the SVAR development was of another aspect of the whole car, the objective certainly being to maintain a reduced drag coefficient and keep the effect of lateral wind forces to a minimum, but also to improve passenger safety in the process. Whilst maintaining the basic qualities of road adhesion and the handling characteristics for which Alfa Romeos were famed, SVAR had

The SVAR Alfasud, with its added side-reinforcing panels clearly visible.

to become impact-safe, or safer, preserving at the same time, as far as possible, the efficiency gains from ESVAR.

A great deal of derision has been aimed at rear spoilers on motor cars, especially large ones such as those fitted by Porsche, these becoming popularly known as 'whale tails' and 'picnic tables'. But methods of persuading air flows to pass *over* cars, instead of under them, and of persuading those airflows to exert downward pressures on the cars during their passage over them, were all part of this combined programme.

Weight penalties imposed in consequence of reinforcing the front and rear ends of the car, as well as the side doors, roof and bonnet, came to some 119lb (54kg). The consequence of this weight addition, though, was a much stronger car for very little penalty in performance. For example, maximum speed remained the same at 115mph (185kph), though 0–60 (0–100) time increased to 10.1 seconds, still better than in the original Alfasud by over half a second. The standing start 1,000 metres time increased by under half a second, but the most important factor from Alfa Romeo's point of view was that the car's average fuel consumption remained the same as ESVAR at almost 36.5mpg (7.7l/

100km) in city traffic, whilst it was 50.2mpg (5.6l/100km) at a constant speed of 56.25mph (90kph) and 55.94mpg (5l/100km) at a constant 75mph (120kph).

Now SVAR had to be subjected to a wide range of tests, to verify its designed-in impact resistance capabilities. It had to resist a glancing blow on the front quarter at 40mph with a barrier angled at 30 degrees, and suffer no doors bursting open or spillage of fuel. The side-impact resistance requirement was severe, in that the car was to resist an impact of 30mph (50kph) with no door opening or body crushing and, again, no fuel spillage. The road tests were next, and the car was put through its paces at Alfa Romeo's Balocco test track to ensure that none of the handling or roadholding qualities had suffered from the experiments.

THE END OF THE ROAD FOR ALFASUD

Much of the work surrounding those Alfasuds found its way into production vehicles over the next few years, part of it being the 16-valve engine already mentioned, along with a developed version

Specification – Alfa Romeo 'Alfa 33' Front-Wheel-Drive Series

Model Alfa 33 Series (FWD)
Year 1983–on

Type 4/5-seat, 5-door saloon and 5-door Station Wagon
Wheelbase 1.3: 2,455mm; all other versions 2,465mm
Track 1.3: 1,392mm (F); 1,359mm (R); 1.3S: 1,397mm (F); 1,364mm (R); 1.5, 1.7 and Station Wagon: 1,367mm (F); 1,364mm (R)
Tyre sizes 165/70SR × 13 (1.3); 175/70R × 13-82T (1.5); 185/60R × 14-82H (1.7 and Sportwagon)
Brakes Disc (F); Drum (R)
Suspension McPherson strut coil front spring and anti-roll bar, rigid axle with A-frame and coil rear springs
Engines 1,350cc/1,490cc/1,712cc sohc to each bank, except 33 16V, which has twin ohc to each bank
No. of cylinders 4 – horizontally opposed
Bore/stroke 1.3: 80mm × 67.2mm; 1.5: 84mm × 67.2mm; 1.7: 87mm × 72.2mm
Induction 1 twin-choke downdraught carburettor on 1.3 & 85bhp 1.5; 2 twin-choke downdraught on other models. Bosch fuel injection on IE and quad-cam (16V) models
Ignition Coil and distributor or electronic system
Power output 1.3: 71bhp @ 6,000rpm 1.5: 85bhp @ 5,800rpm (Gold C/leaf: 95bhp); 1.5TI/Green C/leaf: 105bhp @ 6,000rpm; 1.7: 118bhp @ 6,000rpm; 1.7IE: 110bhp @ 5,800rpm; 1.6v 1.7: 137bhp @ 6,500rpm
Transmission 5-speed transmission in unit with engine, front-wheel drive
Gear ratios 1st 12.195:1; 2nd 7.232:1; 3rd 5.133:1; 4th 3.984:1; 5th 3.313:1; reverse 11.993:1
Versions catalogued Alfa 33 1.3/1.3S Saloon, Alfa 33 1.5 Saloon, Alfa 33 1.5 Gold Cloverleaf Saloon, Alfa 33 1.5 Green Cloverleaf Saloon, Alfa 33 1.5TI Saloon, Alfa 33 1.5 Veloce Saloon, Alfa 33 1.7 Cloverleaf, Alfa 33 1.7 Veloce Saloon, Alfa 33 1.7 Sportwagon, Alfa 33 1.7 Veloce Sportwagon, Alfa 33 1500IE Saloon, Alfa 33 1.7IE Saloon, Alfa 33 Boxer 16V 1.7 Saloon, Alfa 33 B 16V 1.7 Sportwagon

Specification – Alfa Romeo 33 Four-Wheel Drive

Model Alfa 33 4 × 4
Year 1984–on

Type 4/5-seat, 4-door saloon and 5-door Station Wagon
Wheelbase 2,465mm
Track 1,367mm (F); 1,375mm (R)
Tyre sizes 165/70SR × 13 (Saloon), 175/50SR × 13 (Station Wagon)
Brakes Disc (F); drum (R)
Suspension McPherson strut coil spring with anti-roll bar in front, rigid axle with A-frame and coil springs on live rear axle
Engines 1,350cc, 1,490cc single ohc and 1,712cc twin ohc
No. of cylinders 4 – horizontally opposed
Bore/stroke 1.3: 80mm × 67.2mm; 1.5: 84mm × 67.2mm; 1.7: 87mm × 72mm
Induction 2 twin-choke downdraught or fuel injection
Ignition Coil and distributor
Power output 1.3: 71bhp @ 5,800rpm; 1.5: 95bhp @ 5,800rpm; 1.7: 137bhp @ 5,800rpm
Transmission 5-speed transmission in unit with engine and fitted with selectable two/four-wheel drive
Versions catalogued Alfa 33 1.5 4 × 4 Saloon, Alfa 33 1.5 4 × 4 Station Wagon, Alfa 33 1.3 4× 4 Sportwagon, Alfa 33 Permanent 4

of its fuel system and the 'Lamellare' laminar valve introduced into the induction system in some Alfa Romeo engines today. Other gains from this work were included into the body design techniques used in modern times by Alfa Romeo. The Alfa 33 is living proof of those developments but, more particularly, the next generation of Alfa Romeos will gain enormously from the success of those investigations.

The volume production of Alfasuds actually finished, to all intents and purposes, in 1983, though a few odd examples were built, mostly connected with the SVAR and ESVAR programmes, in 1984 and 1985. Just sixteen Alfasuds were built in 1985, all 1350 TI 3-Door Hatchbacks. And then came the new ARNA hatchback . . .

7 A Famous Name Reborn – The Alfetta

FIRST THE SALOON . . .

As the Giulia began to age, a new car, with old ideas, began to form in the minds of the Alfa Romeo Engineering Design team. Handling and roadholding were becoming ever more important to the discerning motorists of the early 1970s, with the result that manufacturers had to be much clearer in their design objectives. One important factor in creating good roadholding is good weight distribution and so the Alfa Romeo team took that point on board and began to consider how they could improve the weight distribution of the Giulia's replacement. Then some bright spark declared that he had the answer, which was to move the gearbox to the rear and have a transaxle.

There is no doubt that the protagonists of front-wheel drive would have tried to laugh that suggestion off the drawing board before it even found its way there. None the less, when someone else pointed out that this was the way the Alfetta 158 and 159 had been built, others began to listen. With the result that the new car, when announced to the motoring world, or press to be more precise, was called the Alfetta Saloon. Like its illustrious forebear, this new car had a de Dion rear axle, with Watts linkages to retain it in place, coil springs and Panhard rods. Front suspension was provided by means of longitudinally placed torsion bars connected to wishbones, with a shock absorber passing through a hole in an upper arm. This arm was connected to a trailing link for fore-and-aft stability.

The engine of the first Alfetta was the familiar 1750 unit, though now it was described as the 1.8, which was slightly more accurate, with it having an actual capacity of 1,779cc. Like the model it was succeeding, the engine was naturally aspirated and, via a 9.5:1 compression ratio, yielded 122bhp. Unlike the earlier models, the clutch was not attached to the engine, but was installed within the gearbox housing, which was rear-mounted, integral with the differential, with drive from the front-mounted engine via an open propellor shaft.

This wasn't the first time an Alfa Romeo production car had been named after a successful racing model, either, for the earlier 1750 had shared the same distinction – though perhaps it wasn't so easily recognizable, as the engine was of virtually 1,750cc capacity. Even so, publicity had played on the link between the current 1750 of the time and its famous pre-war namesake.

THE HATCHBACK REVOLUTION

Coupes had also been on the Alfa Romeo menu for many a long year, but the concept of the hatchback was popularized in the mid-1960s, with the consequence that Alfa Romeo was pressed to think about designing and constructing a three-door hatchback to compete with those already in the market place. Ford was the first company to launch a family coupe, with the Capri, though it very

The Alfetta 1.8 Saloon of 1972.

nearly didn't succeed. The original version of the Capri was a two-door four-seater which, with its 1,600cc engine, was a little underpowered and ponderous. Ford's target market was the young family man who hankered after a sporty car, but had a couple of kids to fit in. Ford finally got it right and then sold hundreds of thousands of Capris, starting a fashion on the way.

Indirectly, a helping hand to the concept of closed 'sporty' cars came from developing American legislation which, with the help of a gentleman named Ralph Nader, was cracking down on open sports cars and convertibles anyway. Their argument was that open cars were potentially dangerous, as there was no protection for the occupants of a car in a rollover situation. So laws were

framed which, whilst not actually banning open cars, made it very difficult to produce them in conformity with safety regulations. The consequence was that a large number of manufacturers abandoned the production of open cars altogether, especially those exporting to the United States, so the coupe gained in popularity.

No sooner had the coupe become the 'in' type of car, than designers began to realize that the rear window could be made into a door, or 'hatch'. The British Reliant company claimed to have pioneered that concept with their Scimitar, though Volvo also reckoned they had pioneered the idea with the P1800. Of British manufacturers, perhaps the best qualified claimant to that distinction is in fact Aston Martin, who hinged the rear

The Aston Martin DB2/4 was one of the first hatchbacks – this was its immediate successor, the DB Mark III, with hatch open.

window of the DB2/4 as long ago as 1953, making it, according to Bentley: 'the fastest shooting brake [an early term for estate car or station wagon] in the world'! Back in the 1950s, a two-door car with an opening rear end was an extreme rarity, but by the 1970s, it was a very different story.

ENTER THE GRAN TURISMO ALFETTA

Alfa Romeo built a reputation for outstanding sporting coupes in the days when other people were putting bodies on their chassis,

but the great success which put them above most of their competition was the Giulietta Sprint of 1954. The courage to produce that model was largely inspired by the earlier success of the 1900 Sprint. So by 1974, with the history of the 1900, the Giulietta, the Giulia, the 1750 and the 2000 Coupes behind them, the Arese team set about introducing a coupe for the 1970s and 1980s. In fact, that car was a hatchback, in the fashion of the day, the Alfetta GT.

A full four-seater, the Alfetta GT was designed, as was its four-door sibling, by Giorgetto Giugiaro of Ital Design. Giugiaro's remit was to produce a car which would

Specification – Alfetta GT, GTV and GTV6 Series

Model Alfetta GT Series
Year 1974–86

Type 4-seat, 3-door hatchback coupes
(1.8, 1.6, 2000, 2.0, 2.0GP, 2.5)
Wheelbase 2,400mm
Track 1,360mm (F) (1,368mm on 2.0
and 2.5); 1,358mm (R)
Tyre sizes 185/70HR × 14; 195/60HR × 15
Brakes Disc on all four wheels
Suspension Longitudinal torsion bar
front with unequal length transverse
links and anti-roll bar, de Dion rear
with Watts linkage and helical coils
Engines 1,779cc/1,570cc/1,962cc dohc or
2,492cc/2,959cc sohc to each bank
No. of cylinders 1.8, 1.6, 2000/2.0: 4 in
line; 2.5/3.0: V-6
Bore/stroke 1.8: 80mm × 88.5mm; 1.6:
78mm × 82mm; 2000/2.0: 84mm ×
88.5mm; V-6 2.5: 88mm × 68.3mm;
V-6 3.0 93mm × 72.6mm
Induction 2 horizontal twin-choke (1.8,
1.6, 2000, 2.0); turbo/2 twin choke
(GTV Turbodelta); fuel injection (GTV6
2.5); 6 downdraught carburettors
(GTV-6 3.0)
Ignition Coil and distributor or
electronic ignition system
Power output 1.8: 122bhp @ 5,500rpm;
1.6: 109bhp @ 5,600rpm; 2000 & 2.0:
130bhp @ 5,400rpm; GTV Turbodelta:
175bhp @ 5,500rpm; GTV6 2.5: 160bhp
@ 5,600rpm
Transmission 5-speed gearbox in unit
with rear axle, driving rear wheels
Gear ratios
  GT 1.8 1st 13.53:1; 2nd 8.20:1; 3rd
5.62:1; 4th 4.264:1; 5th 3.403:1; reverse
12.67:1
  GT 1.6 1st 14.19:1; 2nd 8.60:1; 3rd 5.89:1;
4th 4.472:1; 5th 3.569; reverse 13.287:1
  GTV2000/2 1st 13.53:1; 2nd 8.019:1;
5.515:1; 4th 4.207:1; 5th 3.403:1;
reverse 12.67:1
  GTV Turbo Autodelta 2000 1st
13.53:1; 2nd 8.20:1; 3rd 5.62:1; 4th
4.264:1; 5th 3.403:1; reverse 12.67:1
  GTV6 1st 14.35:1; 2nd 8.019:1; 3rd
5.515:1; 4th 4.207:1; 5th 3.403:1;
reverse 12.67:1

*The distinctive line of the Alfetta GT was
a major design achievement for
Giorgetto Giugiaro.*

satisfy that European standard or 'man plus
wife plus 2.2 kids' in comfort. That car
should also accommodate four adults comfor-
tably, without inflicting on them a condition
known as 'Porsche neck', wherein the rear
seat occupants, after fifteen minutes in the
back seats, emerged looking remarkably like
latter-day emulations of Quasimodo.

Whilst the Alfetta Saloon was of quite a
rounded style, not drastically removed from
Bertone's coupe design – indeed the image of
the Alfetta Saloon has been likened to an
'enlarged' 2000 Sprint – the 'razor-edge' line

Versions catalogued Alfetta GT 1.8,
Alfetta GT 1.6, Alfetta GT SE (Great
Britain only), Alfetta GT 2000, Alfetta
GTV 2.0, Alfetta GTV 2.0 Grand Prix,
Alfetta GTV 2.0 Turbo Autodelta,
Alfetta GTV-6 2.5, Alfetta GTV-6 3.0

Alfetta GT – rear quarter.

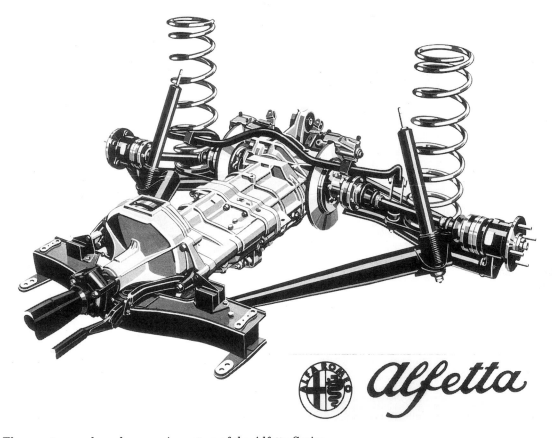

The rear transaxle and suspension set-up of the Alfetta Series.

The Alfetta GT's spacious interior.

A look through the early Alfetta GT shows how the weight distribution was balanced and how roomy the car was.

had become more popular by the early 1970s, giving Giugiaro the opportunity to use a flatter roof and longer line than might have been accepted a decade earlier. The inclusion of a rear hatch, combined with the chopped rear panel, meant that the roof line could allow the rear seat occupants to sit up in comfort, whilst preserving the impression of a true sports coupe.

The year 1974 saw the announcement of the Alfetta GT, in a flurry of publicity which played heavily on its Grand Prix namesake. The wheelbase was 4in (110mm) shorter than the Alfetta Saloon and so successful was Giugiaro's 'architecture' that the 50/50 weight distribution was maintained and a drag coefficient of 0.39 was achieved in wind-tunnel testing. The 1.8-litre engine was used in the first version of the GT, giving a power output of 122bhp at 5,500rpm and a 108mph (174kph) maximum speed. Power was transmitted through the same gearbox as that used in the Saloon, a five-speed unit (with the slightly lower ratio of 1.104:1 instead of 1:1 on fourth) coupled to a 10:41 differential, giving a 4.1:1 final drive. The actual performance of that first Alfetta GT was little different from the Saloon but, packaged as it was, it was destined for instant success.

WIDENING THE RANGE

In characteristic fashion, within a couple of years, the Alfetta GT was available in more than one form. Since the 1,570cc and 1,992cc engines were still available, they were offered in both Alfetta Saloon and GT versions, giving the GT an opening slightly further downmarket. This catered for the enthusiast who wanted image, but couldn't quite afford, or didn't want, the higher performance, higher fuel consumption, road taxes, or higher insurance cost of the larger-engined model. The 2-litre replaced the 1.8 and, with the same transmission ratios, yielded a top road speed of 118mph (190kph).

These two new cars were released upon the world in May 1976, at a special presentation in Florence, the only fundamental difference between them being their respective engine sizes. The 1.6-litre car was to be known as the GT 1.6, whilst the 2-litre was the GTV-2000 (replacing the 2000 GTV of the earlier Bertone coupe, a nomenclature thoroughly confusing to historians).

A few minor cosmetic changes appeared on the Alfetta between 1976 and 1979, but in real terms, it was little changed in those years. However, in 1979, Autodelta, the motor racing organization run by Carlo Chiti for Alfa Romeo (which had produced the Tubolare Zagato coupes and won two world sports car championships), produced a most exciting variant of the Alfetta GTV-2000 by fitting a turbocharger and doing a few minor modifications to the suspension to enable the car to handle the extra power which would result.

The Turbodelta GTV 2.0 was quite a handful, with a power output of over 170bhp for about 0.5 bar boost pressure. The only changes to the outward appearance of the car were: louvre vents to each side of the bonnet, black paint on the bonnet and a yellow, orange, red and blue side stripe with the word 'Autodelta' inscribed upon it. Because Alfa Romeo decided not to pursue this magnificent machine into production, Bell and Colvill, in Great Britain, decided to produce their own Alfa GTV Turbo, using a Garrett Airesearch turbocharger at 0.5 bar, which produced a reported 175bhp.

The year 1980 brought a flurry of changes to the Alfetta GTV. Firstly, the 1.6-litre version was discontinued and a number of cosmetic changes were made which did improve the appearance of the car, cleaning up its lines a little and giving it a new, smaller, radiator grille. Even so, two main variants of the GTV remained in production, with the introduction of an exciting new model. This was the GTV-6 2.5. As its name implies, the new car was powered by a new

The US version, the Alfetta GT 1.8 'America': the bumpers give it away.

Next came the Alfetta GTV 2000.

engine, a V-6 2.5-litre giving 160bhp and a maximum road speed of 130mph (210kph), so completely negating the development work done by Bell and Colvill on their Turbo. Clearly, the British dealer did not know what was coming, but the new car was welcomed by all, as it gave a power boost and a new lease of life to the car.

THE SIX-CYLINDER GTV

The GTV-6's power unit was Alfa Romeo's first-ever V-6 engine, and the first six-cylinder since the demise of the 2600 Series just over a decade earlier. Introduced in the Alfa Six, the car which was designed to return to the market slot vacated by the 2600. It was a superb unit and was destined, in different versions, to serve Alfa Romeo in several cars, from the Six, through the Alfa 90 and the 75, on to the 164 Saloon and the new, exciting Zagato Coupe, the ES30.

This new engine was a departure from Alfa Romeo practice in a number of ways. Not only was it a vee engine, where all their six-cylinder units hitherto had been of in line design, it also had only a single camshaft for each bank of cylinders. It was also configured in a 60 degrees vee, instead of 90 degrees, which had been the angle used by Alfa Romeo in its earlier vee engine design – that used for the Tipo 105/33 sports racing car and developed into the unit for the Montreal coupe. The thinking behind a 60 degree engine was that it would run more smoothly and also fit into the car more easily.

As with the Alfa Six, the original GTV-6 engine was fitted with six Solex carburettors, but realizing that these were a tuner's nightmare, Bosch L-Jetronic fuel injection came to the rescue in the 1980 production version. Brake horsepower of 160 was maintained as the power output of the fuel-injected engine, though the torque rating was down to 157lb/ft at 4,000rpm. The gearbox was the same as that used in the GTV 2.0, though the ratio of fifth gear was

---

Filippo Surace

Filippo Surace is another product of the Turin engineering school; a solid, thinking engineer raised on the unerring power of logic. A native of Reggio Calabria, he was born in 1928 and graduated in 1953 from Turin Polytechnic with a degree in mechanical engineering. It is interesting to note that the subject of his thesis was the automotive application of gas turbine engines. After three years at the Montecatini Study and Research Centre, Surace joined Alfa Romeo at a most exciting time, as the Giulietta was in full production and gaining momentum.

It was Filippo Surace who was at the centre of the project to develop a low-cost replacement for the ageing Alfasud Saloon, by negotiating with the Japanese manufacturer, Nissan. The idea was to take a Japanese car already in production and 'Italianize' it with the Alfasud running gear and badge. This would eliminate the need for expensive press tooling and so preserve capital, something Alfa Romeo desperately needed at the time. The result was the ARNA, which proved to be too 'soggy' to satisfy the established Alfasud clan which had grown up with that car. Sadly, the project was abandoned to Nissan Europe and Surace suffered a lot of flak, unjustifiably. Retaining the mechanical features of the car, Nissan continued its production as the Nissan Cherry Europe for a couple of years, but then it disappeared.

It was Surace, also, who was responsible for the design of the Alfa 33, a car which did finally take off and successfully replaced the Alfasud. He also led the design effort to produce the Alfa 90, a mid-range successor to the Alfetta Saloon, as well as the Alfa 75, the car which today is talked of as a 're-born' Alfa Romeo. If the Alfa 75 were his only true success, then Filippo Surace has earned his place in Alfa Romeo history.

HOW THE ALFA ROMEO GTV6 PERFORMS

Figures taken at 5,268 miles by our own staff at the Motor Industry Research Association proving ground at Nuneaton, and on the Continent.
All Autocar test results are subject to world copyright and may not be reproduced in whole or part without the Editor's written permission.

TEST CONDITIONS:
Wind: 5-15 mph
Temperature: 19 deg C (66 deg F)
Barometer: 29.5 in. Hg (1000.0 mbar)
Humidity: 60 per cent
Surface: dry asphalt and concrete
Test distance: 1,490 miles

MAXIMUM SPEEDS

Gear	mph	kph	rpm
Top (mean)	130	209	5,900
(best)	132	212	6,000
4th	107	172	6,400
3rd	81	130	6,400
2nd	56	90	6,400
1st	31	50	6,400

ACCELERATION

FROM REST

True mph	Time (sec)	Speedo mph
30	2.8	30
40	4.5	40
50	6.3	50
60	8.8	59
70	11.7	68
80	14.7	78
90	19.4	88
100	24.3	97
110	34.6	108

Standing ¼-mile: 16.7 sec, 84 mph
Standing km: 30.6 sec, 107 mph

IN EACH GEAR

mph	Top	4th	3rd	2nd
10-30	—	7.4	5.6	3.4
20-40	10.0	6.9	4.9	3.3
30-50	9.2	6.5	4.7	3.6
40-60	9.4	6.3	4.6	—
50-70	9.7	6.6	5.0	—
60-80	10.4	7.1	5.8	—
70-90	11.3	7.5	—	—
80-100	13.2	9.3	—	—
90-110	17.8	—	—	—

FUEL CONSUMPTION

Overall mpg:
23.2 (12.2 litres/100km)

Constant speed:

Autocar constant speed fuel consumption measurement equipment incompatible with Bosch fuel injection.

Autocar formula:	
Driving	Hard 20.9 mpg.
and conditions	Average 25.5 mpg
	Gentle 30.2 mpg

Grade of fuel: Premium, 4-star (98 RM)
Fuel tank: 16.5 Imp. galls (75 litres)
Mileage recorder reads: 2.0 per cent short

Official fuel consumption figures
(ECE laboratory test conditions; not necessarily related to Autocar figures)
Urban cycle: 19.1 mpg
Steady 56 mph: 36.7 mpg
Steady 75 mph: 28.6 mpg

OIL CONSUMPTION
(SAE 20/50) 800 miles/pint

BRAKING

Fade *(from 84 mph in neutral)*
Pedal load for 0.5g stops in lb

	start/end			start/end
1	12/12	6	20/16
2	20/20	7	24/20
3	20/20	8	24/24
4	20/16	9	32/36
5	24/16	10	28/28

Response *(from 30 mph in neutral)*

Load	g	Distance
10 lb	0.20	150 ft
30 lb	0.48	63 ft
50 lb	0.75	40 ft
70 lb	0.87	35 ft
90 lb	0.98	31 ft
Handbrake	0.40	75 ft

Max. gradient: 1 in 3

CLUTCH
Pedal 30 lb; Travel 5 in.

WEIGHT
Kerb, 24.1 cwt/2,702 lb/1,227 kg
(Distribution F/R, 51.0/49.0)
Test, 27.7 cwt/3,102 lb/1,409 kg
Max. payload 750 lb/340 kg

PRICES

Basic	£7,641.81
Special Car Tax	£625.15
VAT	£1,228.04
Total (in GB)	**£9,495.00**
Seat Belts	Standard
Licence	£70.00
Delivery charge (London)	£126.50
Number plates	£15.00
Total on the Road	**£9,706.50**
(exc. insurance)	

EXTRAS (inc. VAT)
Metallic paint	No extra charge
Manual sunroof	£350.00
Air conditioning	£500.00

TOTAL AS TESTED ON THE ROAD	**£9,706.50**
Insurance	Group not yet available

SERVICE & PARTS
Interval

Change	6,000	12,000	18,000
Engine oil	N/A	N/A	N/A
Oil filter	,,	,,	,,
Gearbox oil	,,	,,	,,
Spark plugs	,,	,,	,,
Air cleaner	,,	,,	,,

Total cost
(Assuming labour at £11.50/hour inc. VAT)

PARTS COST *(including VAT)*
Brake pads (2 wheels) – front	£16.10
Brake pads (2 wheels) – rear	£11.50
Exhaust complete	N/A
Tyre – each (typical)	£89.51
Windscreen	£102.35
Headlamp unit	£36.34
Front wing	£143.75
Rear bumper	£94.30

WARRANTY
12 months/unlimited mileage

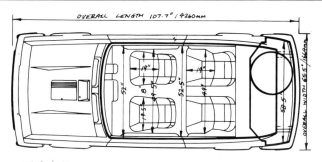

OVERALL LENGTH 107.7"/4260mm
OVERALL WIDTH 65.5"/1664mm
19"
52"
8.5"
53.5"
19"
49"
58.5"

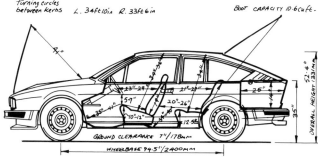

Turning circles between kerbs L. 34ft 10in R. 33ft 6in
BOOT CAPACITY 10.6cu ft.
GROUND CLEARANCE 7"/178mm
WHEELBASE 94.5"/2400mm
FRONT TRACK 54.1"/1374mm
REAR TRACK 53.2"/1351mm
OVERALL HEIGHT 52.4"/133mm
13"-29"
21"-29"
25"
35"
5-7"
20"-26"
10"-12"
12.5"
35"
4"

SPECIFICATION

ENGINE
Head/block	Front, rear drive
	Aluminium alloy/alloy
Cylinders	6 in 60 deg V, wet liners
Main bearings	4
Cooling	Water
Fan	Twin electric
Bore, mm (in.)	88.0 (3.46)
Stroke, mm (in.)	68.3 (2.69)
Capacity, cc in³	2,492 (152.3)
Valve gear	Ohc with pushrod operated exhaust valves
Camshaft drive	Toothed belt
Compression ratio	9.0-to-1
Ignition	Breakerless
Injection	Bosch L-Jetronic
Max power	160 bhp (DIN) at 5,600 rpm
Max torque	157 lb ft at 4,000 rpm

TRANSMISSION
Type	5 speed all indirect transaxle
Clutch	Twin disc diaphragm

Gear	Ratio	mph/1000 rpm
Top	0.780	22.0
4th	1.026	16.7
3rd	1.345	12.7
2nd	1.956	8.8
1st	3.500	4.9

Final drive gear	Hypoid bevel
Ratio	4.1 to 1

SUSPENSION
Front – location	Double wishbones
springs	Longitudinal torsion bars
dampers	Telescopic
anti-roll bar	Yes
Rear – location	De Dion tube, Watts linkage
springs	Coil
dampers	Telescopic
anti-roll bar	Yes

STEERING
Type	Rack and pinion
Power assistance	No
Wheel diameter	15.0 in.
Turns lock to lock	3.6

BRAKES
Circuits	Dual split front/rear
Front	10.5 in. dia. ventilated disc
Rear	9.8 in. dia. disc
Servo	Vacuum
Handbrake	Centre lever rear discs

WHEELS
Type	Alloy
Rim width	6 in.
Tyres – make	Pirelli
– type	P6 radial ply
– size	195/60HR-15
– pressures	F28 R28 psi (normal driving)

EQUIPMENT
Battery	12V 77Ah
Alternator	65A
Headlamps	110/230W halogen
Reversing lamp	Standard
Electric fuses	14
Screen wipers	2-speed, plus intermittent
Screen washer	Electric
Interior heater	Air blending/water valve
Air conditioning	Extra
Interior trim	Cloth seats, cloth headlining
Floor covering	Carpet
Jack	Screw pillar
Jacking points	2 each side
Windscreen	Laminated
Underbody protection	Electrophoretic dip/pvc underbody coating

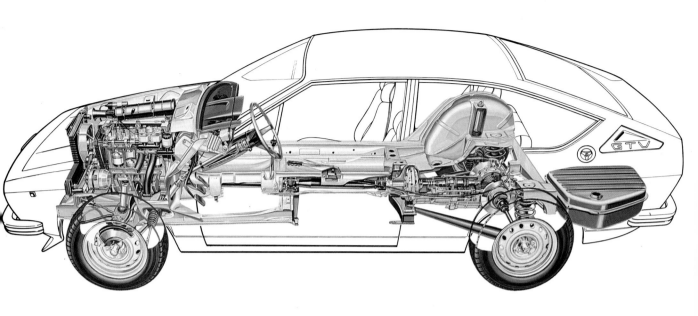

The GTV 2000 'undressed' shows refinement, not change, in the Alfetta Coupe.

The Alfetta GTV 2.0 'Turbodelta' on test.

Front quarter of the Alfetta GTV6 2.5 . . .

. . . and the equally clean rear quarter of the GTV6.

The Alfetta 2.0 engine in cutaway.

Inside the Alfetta GTV6.

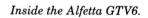

changed from 0.83 to 0.78:1, with the same 4.1:1 final drive.

Now that Alfa Romeo had unleashed such a fiery beast, they had to make it capable of handling the increased power. They fitted larger ventilated front brake discs and wider tyres, to allow it to stop more readily from its quite exciting maximum of 130mph (210kph). This speed brought it quite close to the Porsche 911, though it was a more practical car than its German opponent with its four full seats. As would be expected, handling was quite close to that of the Porsche, too, with 195/65R tyres on Campagnolo wheels.

Styling changes made for the GTV-6 were conferred upon the GTV 2.0, with the virtual disappearance of chrome trim in favour of black; and the newly designed, and much more attractive, coloured bumpers (designed to withstand most American safety legislation as well as being more impact-resistant at all speeds). The interior of the GTV-6 brought changes to the four-cylinder GTV 2.0 as well, in that the dashboard now had all the instruments grouped together, though the speedometer and revolution counter were so positioned as to be very difficult to see at a glance, because the steering wheel was in the way. Gone, though, was the awful reflection of the instruments at night on the interior of the windscreen, thanks to better shrouding.

SPECIAL EDITIONS

Alfa Romeo has often produced special limited edition versions of their cars for specific markets and the Alfetta GT Series went through the same treatment as it became accepted. Often, such special editions are designed to boost flagging sales and this was true of the Alfetta, since the 1979 international fuel crisis, which resulted in a downturn in sales of most commodities throughout the developed world, brought problems for car sales in certain market sectors, too.

The British market has always been a favourite of Alfa Romeo, with a loyal band of enthusiasts for the marque since the 1920s. As a consequence, the GTV-SE was announced, a car based very much on the production model built for North America (named there the 'Sprint Veloce', since Milan thought the Americans would be unlikely to appreciate the connotations of 'Alfetta'). The 'SE' had an identifying badge on the hatchback lid, a vinyl-covered roof in a colour blending with the basic paint finish, a rubbing strip on the doors and body sides and road wheels which were most attractive. These were cast alloy, with a large plain dish face and short spokes connecting to the rim. Velour seat trim was accompanied by a sunroof, electric windows in the doors, spotlamps to the front and rear-mounted fog warning lamps.

Next on the menu of special editions came the GTV 'Strada' (the word meaning 'road'), announced in 1978. Like the GTV-SE, it had velour trim on the inside, electrically powered front windows (remembering that the front half of the rear quarter lights could be lowered) and an electric sunroof. On the outside was a set of cast-alloy wheels of the type used on the earlier Montreal Coupe (these were the kind of wheels which had multiple spokes cast into them to make them look rather like radially spoked wire wheels – nice to look at, but awful to keep clean!). The outside trim was, again like the SE, finished off with a protection strip on the body sides, this time positioned just above the line of the bottom edge of the doors, and a pair of spotlights positioned below the front bumpers.

After the slight re-styling of the 1980 model had settled into the market place, it was time to look at special editions again. So now, for the Italian market only, came the GTV 'Grand Prix' 2.0, produced for 1982. Finished in two-tone red, Alfa Red being the main body colour with striping in a darker colour (though some appear to have escaped with black striping and matching wheels), the exterior of the bodywork differed little from the standard. The words 'Grand Prix' were inserted into the lower body stripe, whilst the bumpers and front air dam were the same colour as the car body, rather than natural black plastic. The wheels were the cast-alloy ones of the normal GTV, except that they were anodized in the stripe colour. On the inside, the detail was much as for the earlier GTV-SE and *Strada* versions, with velour trim and electric windows, though no sunroof.

Coming right up to date, there is a company in Britain today, called Auto Technic, which is offering a very interesting version of the Alfetta GTV-6. They take what they call a 'donor' car and strip it down, performing a total body restoration, with bad metal replaced by new. The engine is also stripped completely and the crankshaft, presuming it to be fit, is reground then fully balanced. Connecting rods are renovated, new pistons fitted and all matched, whilst the manifolds are gas-flowed for maximum efficiency. The engine is then assembled with new camshafts, bearings, cylinder liners, valves, valve guides and ancillaries to make a virtually new engine.

The gearbox and rear axle go through the same kind of treatment and the suspension is lowered. Body trim includes side-skirting, whilst suspension is slightly lowered and tuned to the new 200bhp power output. Interior trim includes Wilton carpeting and leather upholstery, all making this a rather special car for those still well-disposed to the Alfetta for a sum of around £20,000 at the time of writing. Which all goes to show that the Alfetta is still far from dead.

ALFETTA ADVERSARIES

Competitors for the Alfetta GTs were numerous, though surprisingly few offered directly comparative specification or performance. For example, starting from the lowest end of the market, to compare with the Alfetta GT 1.6 there was Britain's Morris Marina Coupe, a 1.8-litre engined vehicle with very comparable interior dimensions and space, but it wasn't a hatchback and offered nowhere near the performance or handling – in fact, it was the epitome of the 'boy-racer-with-leather-gloves-and-nothing-else' element of motoring. The Ford Capri 1600 was a hatchback and, with its 2,600mm wheelbase, was able to offer reasonable passenger space, but didn't. The rear

The Alfetta and Its Adversaries							
Car and Model	Engine Type and Size	Gearbox	Max. Speed		Consumption		GB Price
			mph	(kph)	mpg	l/100km	
Alfa Romeo Alfetta GT 1.8	1,779cc 4-cylinder twin ohc	5-speed	115	(185)	24–28	(12–10)	£3,125 (1974)
Lotus Elan Plus 2S	1,558cc 4-cylinder twin ohc	5-speed	118	(190)	26–30	(11–9)	£2,789 (1974)
Mazda RX4 Coupe	2,292cc twin-rotor Wankel rotary	4-speed	104	(167)	22–24	(13–12)	£2,050 (1974)
MGB-GT 1800 Coupe	1,798cc 4-cylinder pushrod ohv	4-speed	106	(170.5)	23–29	(12–10)	£2,659 (1975)
Morris Marina 1.8 Coupe	1,798cc 4-cylinder pushrod ohv	4-speed	95	(155)	28–30	(10–9)	£2,147 (1975)
Alfa Romeo Alfetta GT 1.6	1,570cc 4-cylinder twin ohc	5-speed	106	(170.5)	24–26	(12–11)	£3,970 (1976)
Ford Capri 1600 S Coupe	1,593cc 4-cylinder single ohc	4-speed	98	(154)	28–30	(10–9)	£2,307 (1975)
Alfa-Romeo Alfetta GTV-2000	1,962cc 4-cylinder twin ohc	5-speed	115	(185)	24–28	(12–10)	£5,499 (1977)
Porsche 911S 2.4 Coupe	2,341cc flat-6 air-cooled twin ohc	5-speed	130	(209)	26–32	(11–9)	£6,235 (1973)
Alfa Romeo Alfetta GTV-6 2.5	2,492cc V-6 single ohc per bank	5-speed	130	(209)	22–26	(13–11)	£8,400 (1980)
Ford Capri 3.0 Coupe	2,698cc V-6 pushrod ohv	5-speed	120	(195)	24–26	(12–11)	£5,857 (1980)
Reliant Scimitar GTE	2,994cc V-6 pushrod ohv	5-speed	110	(175)	23–25	(12–11)	£8,137 (1980)
MGB GT V8 Coupe	3,528cc V-8 pushrod ohv	4-speed	122	(196)	20–25	(14–11)	£5,699 (1979)
Porsche 911 3.0 Coupe	2,998cc flat-6 air-cooled twin ohc	5-speed	143	(230)	24–32	(12–9)	£14,934 (1979)

passengers were cramped for legroom, and headroom was more limited than the Alfetta, too. This same problem carries over, of course, to the larger-engined Capris, so whilst they have better performance, they are still no match for the Alfetta.

The GTV-6 had no more adversaries than its smaller-engined sibling, since the only two that offered a real contest were put out of reach on the grounds of price alone. For example, the Ferrari Dino 308 was almost double the price for a 3-litre engine and 150mph (240kph) performance, with cramped and deaf rear passengers. The 2.7-litre Porsche 911 had a similar rear passenger problem, but was a more predictable, and perhaps more exciting, ride. The also-rans featured the Ford Ghia Capri, the MGB GT-V8, the Reliant Scimitar GTE and the Mazda RX4. But to an *Alfista*, there is no substitute for Alfa Romeo.

FAREWELL TO THE GTV

By 1985, the Alfa Romeo GTV 2.0 and GTV-6

The Alfetta GTV 2.0 'Grand Prix', a special edition available only in Italy.

The AutoTechnic GTV-200, a specialist re-build based on the GTV6 2.5.
An elegant variation on a magnificent theme.

were discontinued from production, with no direct replacement. New on the horizon was the Alfa 75 Saloon, this time offered from scratch in several versions; but no coupe. Development and production cash were becoming scarce, so there was no immediate prospect of a successor to the Alfetta for some time to come. But then, along came Fiat and new development resources. Now, the *Alfisti* have something to look forward to, for the new corporate image for the 1990s is high profile. The Type ES30 Sprint Zagato has appeared, albeit in limited numbers, which certainly augurs well for the future of the coupe.

If we need any further confirmation that the coupe is here to stay in Alfa Romeo's eyes, then look at the revelation of the 1991 Geneva Motor Show. Here was revealed not just another new Alfa Romeo coupe in the mould of the SZ, but another totally new concept in the form of a four-wheel-drive super coupe – the Alfa 164 Coupe. Not destined for production (they said that initially about the SZ), this new model introduced all-wheel drive to sporting Alfas for the first time. Equipped with the 3-litre Cloverleaf engine, now producing 240bhp, this latest Alfa concept car was expected to have a maximum speed of around 155mph (250kph) and is being used as a test-bed for the development of high performance four-wheel-drive systems.

Of course, the 33 Permanent 4 precedes the 164 into any level of production as a four-wheel-drive sports car, but just looking at the specification on paper of this latest 'Super Car' sets the adrenalin going. After all, what is Alfa Romeo without at least one Super Coupe in the cupboard?

8 Coupes for All – The Alfasud Sprint and the Sprint

After producing the Alfetta GT Coupe, Giorgetto Giugiaro was given the task of designing another coupe, this one for greater volume manufacture and with front-wheel drive, thus using the Alfasud floorpan. It was felt at Arese that there was a market out there for a smaller coupe which might take the place of the original Giulietta Sprint, the Alfetta being seen as a larger car. Surprisingly perhaps, the Alfasud-Sprint (when it came) was no smaller in overall dimensions than its rear-wheel-drive sibling.

From behind, the Sprint is identifiably different from the Alfetta GTV but clearly of the same design family.

It was in 1976 that the new version of the Alfasud arrived in the market place. It received a warm welcome, as many motoring correspondents had expressed the view, gleaned from the market, that there was a place for just such a car. This new model was a three-door hatchback, preceding the hatchback saloon by six years. Being a three-door and having a hatch which was little larger than the rear window, the body shell was much stronger than the Alfasud Saloon: attention had been paid to the proven weak spots of the saloon version. The rear quarter panel was a major contributor to body rigidity, whilst the rear seats did not fold down in the true fashion of hatchbacks.

Many take the view that the Alfasud Sprint was a more attractive body design than that of the Alfetta GT, with its slightly flatter roof-line giving the impression of a lower, longer car. It was slightly lower, though not quite as long as the Alfetta, and was somewhat lighter. Powered by the original 1,286cc version of the 1.3-litre engine, it is hardly surprising that the Alfasud Sprint relied more on its aerodynamic penetration than sheer power to propel it to its maximum 103mph (165kph). But here it was, a new Sprint coupe, produced in the spirit of the Giulietta (which, incidentally, had a 1,290cc power unit in its first form) and aimed at Alfa Romeo's volume market sector – at the young family man who wanted a sporting car with four seats and at the more mature individual who wanted a practical leisure vehicle with not too much power and not too big a price tag.

A CAR FOR ALL SEASONS

Like the Alfasud Saloon prototypes, the new Sprint Coupe was tested all over Europe, to ensure that it would give design performance in all markets at which it was targeted. The

---

Specification – Alfasud Sprint/ Alfa Romeo Sprint Coupe

Model Alfasud Sprint/ Alfa Romeo Sprint
Year 1976–84, 1984–89

Type 4-seat, 3-door hatchbacks
Wheelbase 1976–79: 2,450mm; 1980-on: 2,455mm
Track
 Between 1976 and 1979 1,380mm (F); 1,350mm (R)
 Between 1980 and 1989 1,392mm (F); 1,359mm (R)
Tyre sizes 165/70SR × 13 Alfasud Sprint; 185/60HR × 14 82H Sprint/Veloce (also 185/55HR–340)
Brakes Disc on all four wheels up to 1987, thereafter disc front/drum rear as on Alfa 33
Suspension McPherson strut coil spring with anti-roll bar in front, rigid axle, longitudinal tie-rods and coil springs at rear
Engines 1,286cc; 1,350cc; 1,490cc; 1,712cc single ohc per bank
No. of cylinders 4 horizontally opposed
Bore/stroke 80mm × 64mm (1,286), 80mm × 67.2mm (1,350), 84mm × 67.2mm (1,500), 87mm × 72mm (1,712)
Induction Single downdraught twin-choke on Alfasud Sprint; 2 twin-choke downdraught Alfasud Sprint Veloce, Alfa Romeo Sprint & Sprint Veloce
Ignition Coil and distributor
Power output 76bhp @ 6,000rpm (1,286cc); 86bhp @ 6,000rpm (1,350cc); 95bhp @ 5,800rpm (1,500cc); 118bhp @ 5,800rpm (1,712cc)
Transmission 5-speed transmission in unit with engine, front-wheel drive
Gear ratios 1st 14.59:1; 2nd 8.47:1; 3rd 5.88:1; 4th 4.60:1; 5th 3.82:1; reverse 12.70:1
Versions catalogued Alfasud Sprint, Alfasud Sprint Veloce 1.3, Alfasud Sprint Veloce 1.5, Alfasud Sprint Veloce Plus 1.5, Alfasud Sprint Veloce Saloon, Alfasud Sprint Veloce Trofeo, Alfasud Sprint Quadrifoglio, Alfasud Sprint Green Cloverleaf 1.5, Alfa Romeo Sprint Green Cloverleaf 1.5, Alfa Romeo Sprint 1.7, Alfa Romeo Sprint Veloce 1.7

*Whilst Giugiaro designed the production Sprint, he also designed this little bit
of nonsense, called the 'Caimano' Sprint.*

*Once inside, the rear seat occupant has more
room than in many sporting coupes.*

floorpan was directly taken from the Alfasud
Saloon and the 1,300cc engine was specially
developed for the new model, though of
course, it appeared in the TI Saloon as well as
the coupe, so as to provide a ready volume
potential for engine production.

For a three-door sporty hatchback, the
Sprint was a remarkably roomy car, capable
of seating four adults in comfort, five at a
pinch. Of course, long doors were a bit of a
problem in most cars, so Alfa Romeo had to
give some attention to making sure that on
this car, they were hinged with sufficient
support to enable them to open and close
without dropping after a very short period.
Also, body strength and rigidity were

important, especially on the hinge posts and rear door shut plates. As usual, the designers made the car with too little headroom for very tall drivers, but most found the access, seating space, legroom and steering wheel reach reasonably comfortable, though the typically Italian-long-arm driving position prevailed.

Like the Saloon, the Alfasud Sprint stuck to the road very well and cornered as though on rails, which quickly endeared it to its owners. With the five-speed gearbox and the same gearing as the TI Saloon, the new coupe was shod with 165/70-13 tyres, instead of the 145-13s of the TI, giving the same speed per

Here's a cutaway of the twin-carburettor Sprint engine (note the twin cam lobes, which were abandoned for single lobes and shim adjustment in Series 3).

This is the Alfasud Sprint Veloce 1.5 Second Series.

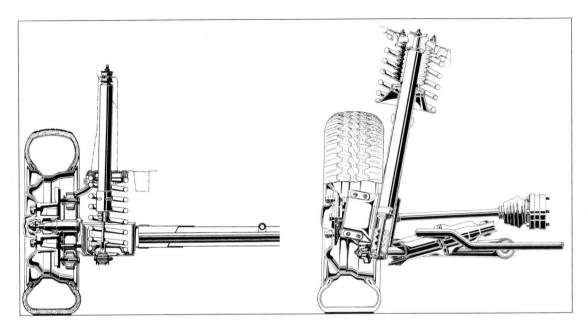

These two drawings, showing the Sprint suspension, tell something of the car's legendary roadholding and cornering ability.

thousand revolutions of the engine in top gear, at 17.4mph (28kph) per thousand. However, with the Sprint having to contend with a higher weight of 17cwt (865kg), the TI reached 50mph (80kph) fractionally quicker than the coupe, though the Sprint had a slightly higher top speed, thanks to its better aerodynamic shape and lower drag coefficient.

THE SERIES ONE AND SERIES TWO CARS

Early road tests tell us that the original series of Alfasud Sprint, with its 1,286cc engine, was in the mould of all new Alfa Romeo models up to that time, in that it was not endowed with particularly sparkling performance, but that it demonstrated immediately its potential for development. As the bugs were ironed out, so the car was developed and, in 1978 (in Britain, at least),

the next phase of Alfasud Sprint came on to the market, in the form of the 1,490cc-engined version.

The Sprint 1.5 was still a Series 1 car in its earliest form. Introduced into Britain in March 1978, it improved on the top speed by only 2mph (3kph) but its 0–60mph (0–100kph) time was improved by more than a full second, to 11.2 seconds. This was quite a respectable time in its day, though perhaps nothing special in the last decade of the Twentieth Century. General performance was, however, considered to be quite good for its time and the roadholding made up for a great deal, as this was well the equal of many a more expensive vehicle from anywhere else in Europe.

In designing the Alfasud, Giorgetto Giugiaro had a great deal of valuable experience upon which to draw. He already knew what Alfa Romeo would accept and expect of him, working on the experience of the Alfetta GT. He knew they would accept a 'junior version'

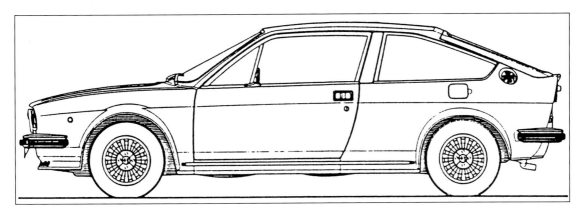

The top drawing shows the clean profile and the lower one the solid structure of the Sprint body shell.

of that car and he knew, having already performed a similar exercise on the Alfetta, that the company would accept a car which had only its floorpan in common with the Saloon version. The other sphere of experience which equipped him well to deal with the front-wheel-drive coupe concept was that he had already designed and developed the Volkswagen Scirocco, which had been widely praised and accepted by a public

ager for this type of car. In styling terms, the Alfasud Sprint was an advance on the Scirocco, blended with features of the Alfetta to identify it as an Alfa Romeo.

Inside the Alfasud Sprint, the standard of trim was everything the Alfa Romeo enthusiast had come to expect. Instrumentation was all in a single binnacle, with a matching speedometer and revolution counter on either side of it and the water

The original Alfasud Sprint 1.3 Coupe.

*These two pictures show a very exciting and special Sprint variant, the
Sprint 6C. Built as a one-off experiment, it was powered by a rear-mounted
Alfa 6 engine and was very fast!*

thermometer and oil pressure gauge placed
between the larger two instruments. The
deeply dished three-spoke steering wheel
had a rather slender rim against modern
standards and presented the usual long-arm/
short-leg driving position. Perhaps the most
irritating feature which the Sprint inherited
from its saloon sibling was the closely
positioned pedals with nowhere to rest the
left foot in comfort away from the clutch
pedal.

Ventilation of this Alfasud coupe left a
little to be desired on a cool damp day, as the
windscreen would mist up without the power
assistance of the fan and the side windows
were little better when there were four in the
car. However, it was possible to open the door

windows very slightly, and the rear quarter
lights could also be opened by rotating a
screw-down knob, though arthritic or very
young fingers found this no easy task, as the
knob was quite stiff to turn.

All this said, the Alfasud Sprint was an
exciting looking car, with a performance
well-matched to its target market and price
tag. Luggage space was excellent for the
young family or the couple who occasionally
carried additional passengers. The rather
heavy tailgate was supported by two gas
struts and the luggage compartment was
covered by a soft roll-up panel which was
located on to the side valances of the
compartment by means of Velcro strips, a
very neat idea, if one which called for regular

cleaning of fluff and debris from the sticky patches. Stiffening of this soft panel was by means of a sequence of small-diameter bars threaded through the width of it. It is interesting to note that the luggage space in the Sprint is larger than that of either the Alfetta GT or of the Alfasud Saloon and somewhat larger than many family cars.

When the Series 2 Sprint Veloce was introduced, it came with an improved performance, both over its predecessor and over the new TI Saloon which followed it. Now, the Sprint, with an uprated 1.5 engine, was capable of giving 109mph (175kph) top speed and a 0–60mph (0–100kph) time of 10.2 seconds. This was a full second off the 0–60mph (0–100kph) time of the earlier Sprint 1.5, as well as a 6mph (10kph) improvement on top speed. The Sprint Veloce was truly an Alfa Romeo and was probably the Alfasud version which did more

to convince the die-hards of the merits of the flat-four engined models.

In the first year of production (1976) there were just under 2,200 Sprint 1.3s built, increasing by more than 600 per cent to 12,046 for 1977, whilst 1978 saw a fall in 1.3 production to just over 4,000 bringing the total production to 18,356. The Sprint 1.5, on the other hand, went into reasonable quantity production straight away, with over 14,400 built in 1978, falling to a few more than 11,250 in 1979 and just 122 in 1980, bringing its total production run to 25,823. Additional to these figures came the 1,351cc-engined Sprint, which went into production in 1978, though its production in the two years it was on offer was quite modest, there being just over 2,800 built in the total run, 1,675 of those produced in 1979.

Looking at these production figures with

hindsight, one is drawn to conclude that the Alfasud Sprint might not have been a particularly successful model, based upon the numbers built. However, one has to realize that Alfa Romeo was not the kind of volume car maker who had to make hundreds of thousands of a car for it to be considered a successful product. It may certainly be that they had hoped for large numbers, but on the other hand, if the car was not considered successful, then it is certain that Alfa Romeo would have cut their losses and discontinued the Sprint much earlier, and not proceeded with the Series 3 range. On the other hand, the Alfasud Sprint was produced in somewhat larger numbers than either of the early Alfetta GTs.

THE SPRINT GOES ON

There were more Sprint Veloces produced than any other variant of the model and by the end of 1983, some 41,281 had been built, bringing the total production run of all Sprint Coupe variants up to that year end to just over 100,000. With styling and quality improvements, the Series 3 range was poised to take over the Sprint's market position and continue in production until 1989.

Series 3 began with the introduction of the Sprint Veloce Plus in 1981. This was a 1.5 version, with the now-familiar performance figures and a slightly improved interior. The exterior changed little in this period and continued, with the odd example of side-striping and minor changes with the 1982 models of Sprint Veloce and Sprint Trofeo — the Trofeo marking the promotion of the Alfasud Sprint Trophy one-model race series.

For 1983 came the Sprint Speciale, a 1.5 model with improved interior trim and modified dashboard and venting. A leather-rimmed steering wheel came into the specification and by the end of that year, the name of the Sprint Series was changed to remove the 'Alfasud'. This was to coincide

with the demise of the Alfasud Saloon range and the Sprints now became known simply as Alfa Romeo Sprint models. By now, all traces of chrome exterior metal trim had disappeared, to be replaced with black trims. The bumpers and radiator grille were now made from black plastic material and the familiar Alfa Romeo radiator grille shape was in silver colour or green (for the 'Quadrifoglio Verde' or Green Cloverleaf model).

As the Alfa 33 took over the role of the Alfasud and Arna Saloons, so thoughts turned to standardization of design features and components. As a consequence of this, the Sprint assumed the braking system of the 33, with disc front brakes and drums at the rear, the diagonally split system being designed to ensure continued braking if one line failed. In the engine, the camshaft design had already changed, switching from the dual-lobe cams with an adjuster set-screw between them to a more orthodox single-lobe design which was now adjusted by means of shims of predetermined thicknesses being placed between the bucket tappets and the camshaft.

The camshaft change was made because many engines had experienced camshaft problems as the result of poor routine inspection and subsequent poor maintenance. Specifically, if camshaft bearings wore and adjustments were not properly made to tappet clearances, then the two cam lobes were found to wear quite quickly and sometimes not at a constant rate, which led to all kinds of mechanical problems.

By 1986, the Alfa Sprint was beginning to gasp for breath whilst trying to keep up with many of its less illustrious competitors. As a consequence, Alfa Romeo engineers decided that another enlargement of engine was justified and in the following year, they introduced the largest flat-four version yet: the 1,712cc 1.7 engine, which produced 118bhp at 5,800rpm or, translated into road speed, 125mph (200kph).

Two special Sprints, the Sprint Trofeo...

...and another, the Sprint Veloce.

ALFA ROMEO SPRINT GREEN CLOVERLEAF

SPECIFICATION

ENGINE
Longways front, front-wheel drive.
Head/block Al. alloy/cast iron. 4 cylinders horizontally opposed, bored block/3 main bearings. Water cooled, electric fan.
Bore 84.0mm (3.36in.), stroke 67.2mm (2.65in.), capacity 1,490 c.c. (91.0 cu. in.).
Valve gear ohc, toothed-belt camshaft drive. Compression ratio 9.5 to 1.
Electronic breakerless ignition, twin-choke downdraught carburettors.
Max power 105 bhp (PS-DIN) (78kW ISO) at 6,000 rpm. Max torque 98 lb. ft. at 4,000 rpm.

TRANSMISSION
Five-speed manual. Single dry plate clutch, 7.9 in. dia.

Gear	Ratio	mph/1,000 rpm
Top	0.82	18.7
4th	1.03	15.0
3rd	1.39	11.1
2nd	2.05	7.5
1st	3.75	4.1

Final drive gear hypoid, ratio 4.10.

SUSPENSION
Front, independent, MacPherson strut, coil springs, telescopic dampers, anti-roll bar. Rear, dead axle, trailing arms, coil springs, telescopic dampers.

STEERING
Rack and pinion. Steering wheel diameter 15in., 3.6 turns lock to lock.

BRAKES
Dual circuits, split front/rear. Front 10.2in. (258mm) dia. discs. Rear 9.2in. (233mm) dia. discs. Vacuum servo. Handbrake, centre lever acting on front discs.

WHEELS
Al. alloy, 5.5in. rims. Tyres (Michelin TRX on test car), size 190/55HR-340, pressures F 26, R 24 psi (Normal driving).

EQUIPMENT
Battery 12V, 43Ah. Alternator 45A. Headlamps 110W. Reversing lamp standard. 14 electric fuses. 2-speed, plus intermittent/screen wipers. Electric screen washer. Air-blending interior heater. Cloth seats, cloth headlining, carpet with heel mat floor covering. Scissor jack; two jacking points each side. Laminated windscreen.

DIMENSIONS

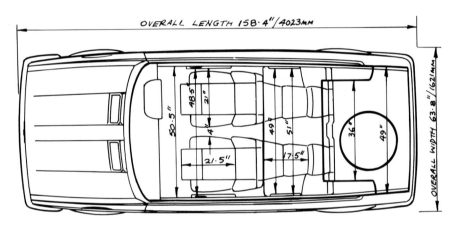

Turning circles: Between kerbs L.13ft 10in R 34ft 4in

Boot capacity 11.6 cu ft

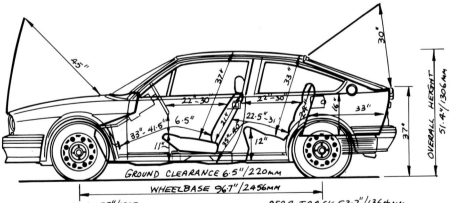

PERFORMANCE

MAXIMUM SPEEDS

Gear	mph	kph	rpm
OD Top (mean)	107	172	5,750
(best)	111	179	5,950
4th	98	158	6,500
3rd	74	119	6,500
2nd	51	82	6,500
1st	27	43	6,500

ACCELERATION

	True mph	Time (sec)	Speedo mph
FROM REST	30	3.6	31
	40	5.3	41
	50	7.6	52
	60	10.8	62
	70	14.6	72
	80	20.1	83
	90	27.1	93
	100	42.6	105
	110	—	113

Standing ¼-mile: 18.0sec, 77 mph
Standing km: 33.5sec, 95 mph

	mph	Top	4th	3rd	2nd
IN EACH GEAR	10-30	—	10.1	6.5	4.0
	20-40	11.9	8.7	5.8	3.8
	30-50	11.5	8.1	5.7	4.2
	40-60	12.0	8.5	6.1	—
	50-70	13.6	9.3	7.1	—
	60-80	15.5	10.1	—	—
	70-90	18.3	12.2	—	—
	80-100	27.7	—	—	—

FUEL CONSUMPTION

Overall mpg:
13.9 (11.8 litres/100km) 5.3 mpl

Constant speed:

mph	mpg	mpl	mph	mpg	mpl
30	48.6	10.7	70	32.5	7.2
40	45.7	10.1	80	29.1	6.4
50	42.7	9.4	90	23.2	5.1
60	37.6	8.3	100	18.2	4.0

Autocar formula: Hard 21.5 mpg
Driving and Average 26.3 mpg
conditions Gentle 31.1 mpg

Grade of fuel: Premium, 4-star (98 RM)
Fuel tank: 11 Imp. galls (50 litres)
Mileage recorder reads: 2.1 per cent long

OIL CONSUMPTION

(SAE 10W/50) 2,000 miles/litre

BRAKING

Fade *(from 77mph in neutral)*
Pedal load for 0.5g stops in lb

	start/end		start/end
1	38/42	6	44/52
2	36/42	7	44/52
3	36/48	8	48/50
4	40/56	9	44/50
5	44/50	10	48/56

Response *(from 30 mph in neutral)*

Load	g	Distance
20lb	0.21	143ft
40lb	0.44	68ft
60lb	0.67	45ft
80lb	0.72	42ft
110lb	0.84	35.8ft
Handbrake	0.20	151ft

Max gradient: see text

CLUTCH Pedal 28lb; Travel 5.5in.

WEIGHT

Kerb, 19.1cwt/2,148lb/974kg
Distribution F/R, 61.6/38.4)
Test; 22.4cwt/2,513lb/1,140kg
Max. payload, 882lb/400kg

TEST CONDITIONS:

Wind: 19-30 mph
Temperature: 5 deg C (41 deg F)
Barometer: 29in. Hg (985 mbar)
Humidity: 82 per cent
Surface: damp asphalt and concrete
Test distance: 948 miles

Figures taken at 10,325 miles by our own staff at the Motor Industry Research Association proving ground at Nuneaton. All Autocar test results are subject to world copyright and may not be reproduced in whole or part without the Editor's written permission.

This final phase in the development of the Sprint series featured only detail changes to the exterior in the basic model, which was the Sprint 1.7 Coupe. These details included a rear spoiler across the back of the hatch, colour-matched door mirrors and re-designed (easier to clean) road wheels. Inside, the car was much as before, with the dashboard being the same as its immediate predecessor. Upholstery was now finished in a fine dog-tooth check woven cloth, with reinforcing vinyl panels in the high-wear areas, whilst the centres of the head restraints were filled in with a cloth-faced padding to match the seat covering.

The other model was the Alfa Romeo Sprint Veloce, which was now equipped with a body streamlining kit and five-spoke wheels. The body kit consisted of the spoiler common to both versions, a pair of side-skirts

The 1983–85 Alfa Romeo Sprint Green Cloverleaf 1.5.

The Sprint Veloce 1.5 Green Cloverleaf showing the revamped radiator grille, which gives the car a whole new look.

fitted to the door sills and a deep front air dam. Bumpers were colour-keyed to the paintwork, in the current fashion, though what all this extra trim did for the performance is dubious, especially since Alfa Romeo quoted the same performance figures for both models. Inevitably, however, the Veloce was set at a higher price, appealing no doubt to the 'boy racer' fraternity.

END OF THE LINE

The year 1988 saw the last series of appearances for the Alfa Romeo Sprint on the international motor show circuit. At the Turin show, there was a new 'Boxer' engine on display, which led to speculation as to whether the last breath of life of the Sprint's production might be brought to it by this engine. It was a quad-cam four-cylinder, with a power output of 'around 140bhp', to quote factory figures. With that kind of power, it certainly would have called for some changes to the front suspension, but what an exciting car it would have made the Sprint. However, in characteristic Alfa Romeo fashion, no commitment was made as to when, even if, or in what car the 1,712cc quad-cam boxer unit would become available.

Finally, everybody was put out of their misery and told quite specifically that the new four-cam engine was *not* destined for the

The final version of the Sprint was the 1.7 Veloce, with side-skirting and an added rear spoiler.

Sprint Coupe and that it would not be in production before 1990. So the Sprint continued in production as it was into 1989, giving the engineering team a chance to improve and develop the 33 Saloon. When, reluctantly, Alfa Romeo had to admit the Sprint was becoming a little long in the tooth and was no longer selling in sufficient numbers to warrant remaining in the catalogue, it was brought to the end of its thirteen-year production run in 1989.

Speculation continues about the Sprint since, whilst the 1976 Giugiaro design is now a little *passé*, there remains a very sporty engine of great potential waiting for a suitable coupe body to occupy. In interviews with Giovanbattista Razelli, the press have extracted hints of Zagato-style coupes going into volume production. This has raised the question: 'Is there likely to be a front-wheel-drive Zagato with the quad-cam engine?'. It would certainly be a truly exciting car, if that were to be so.

Until Alfa Romeo publishes its intentions, we can only wait and see – and hope that the 'Boxer' will ultimately find its way into a suitable successor to the Sprint. In the meantime, the Sprint itself is 'classic' material and is set to become another sought-after model in the enthusiast market, especially as the values of the Alfetta GTVs increase beyond the reach of driving enthusiasts. However, the Sprint deserves its own accolades, for it *is* a fine car and *does* give a lot of fun and satisfaction to its owners, as has virtually every Alfa Romeo before it.

COMPETITORS TO THE SPRINT

In the early days of the Alfa Sprint, its only real adversary was the Volkswagen Scirocco – and this had as much to do with the similarity of appearance as anything else. That similarity was to be expected, when the model profile delivered to Giorgetto Giugiaro from Wolfsburg was very similar to that which came to him from Alfa Romeo. Both were to be three-door hatchbacks with four full seats and front-wheel drive – cars to appeal to the young sporting family man who could no longer use a two-seater.

The principal differences between the Scirocco and the Sprint were the charisma of the names and the drive-train. The VW was a transverse engine installation, whilst the Alfa Romeo was longitudinally in line, and, of course, Alfa Romeo was a name synonymous with sporting cars. However, there was a price tag difference, too, and that made the difference to the production volumes. The VW won hands down, but sold more in

Car and Model	Engine Type and Size	Gearbox	Max. Speed		Consumption		GB Price
			mph	(kph)	mpg	l/100km	
Alfasud Series 1.3	1,286cc flat-4 single ohc per bank	5-speed	105	(170)	24–26	(12–11)	£3,999 (1977)
Volkswagen Scirocco Coupe	1,588cc 4-cylinder single ohc	5-speed	120	(195)	30–33	(9–8.5)	£3,140 (1977)
Opel Manta 1600 Coupe	1,584cc 4-cylinder single ohc	4-speed	91	(146)	25–33	(11–8.5)	£2,843 (1977)
Lancia Beta HPE Coupe	1,592cc 4-cylinder single ohc	5-speed	107	(172)	23–32	(12–9)	£3,545 (1976)
Alfasud Sprint Veloce 1.5	1,490cc flat-4 single ohc per bank	5-speed	106	(170.5)	24–26	(12–11)	£5,165 (1979)
Matra-Simca Bagheera Coupe	1,442cc 4-cylinder pushrod ohv	5-speed	105	(170)	28–30	(10–9)	£5,310 (1977)
Colt Celeste Coupe	1,597cc 4-cylinder single ohc	5-speed	102	(164)	26–32	(11–9)	£2,750 (1977)
Alfa Romeo Sprint Veloce 1.7	1,712cc flat-4 single ohc per bank	5-speed	118	(190)	26–30	(11–9)	£10,200 (1989)
Volvo 480ES Coupe	1,721cc 4-cylinder single ohc	5-speed	109	(175)	26–29	(11–10)	£12,175 (1989)
Audi Quattro Coupe 1.8	1,781cc 4-cylinder single ohc	5-speed	115	(185)	26–29	(11–10)	£17,393 (1989)
Porsche 924S Coupe	2,479cc 4-cylinder single ohc	5-speed	137	(220)	26–32	(11–9)	£21,923 (1988)
Nissan 200SX Turbo Coupe	1,809cc 4-cylinder single ohc	5-speed	140	(225)	28–32	(10–9)	£18,096 (1990)

The Sprint Veloce.

Germany, the Benelux and Nordic countries, whilst Alfa Romeo retained its business base in southern Europe and Great Britain.

Cars which have, along the line, challenged the Alfa Sprint have included Britain's Lotus Elan +2S (and later, the Esprit), MGB-GT 1800, France's Matra Simca Bagheera, Germany's Opel Manta and Porsche 912 coupes, Italy's Fiat 128 Sport and Lancia Beta HPE, Japan's Mazda RX-7 and Colt Celeste. All were coupes; some had hatchbacks, some had not. Most did not offer a direct comparison in performance, accommodation *and* price, the Lancia Beta and the Colt Celeste perhaps coming nearest.

Perhaps the biggest challenge to the Alfa Romeo Sprint, and cars of its kind, comes from the massive improvement in performance and handling characteristics of the smaller family saloons of the late 1980s and those coming in the last decade of this century, such as the British Rover 214SLi. This one car, as an example, has a maximum speed of well over 100mph (160kph) handling the equal of many a sports coupe and comfort to suit the most demanding family. Fuel consumption and acceleration match most 2-litre cars and it is not expensive. It is this kind of car which has motivated Alfa Romeo to introduce such vehicles as the Alfa 33 Quadrifoglio 16-valve, which has ultimately become the home for the quad-cam boxer engine. But it isn't quite the same. There's still a market niche for a four-seat three-door hatchback coupe and Alfa Romeo could fill it with a new and truly exciting Alfa 33 Sprint Coupe, perhaps with four-wheel drive to make it the first-ever four-wheel-drive sporting Alfa in volume production.

9 The Spider Grows Up

Beginning in the late 1960s, there was a distinct downturn in sales of open sports cars, to the point that, by the mid-1970s, sporting coupes dominated the enthusiast sector of the market. American safety legislation was as much behind the demise in popularity of open sports cars as anything else and even Alfa Romeo's principal British competitor, the Lotus Elan, was being offered for 1969 as a fixed-head coupe with a 105bhp 1,600cc engine, along with its Elan +2 sibling. These were fine cars which, with much-improved reliability, were better placed to compete, but the open Elan was being played down in favour of the protection of a roof. Morgan continued with the Plus Four, adding the Rover V-8 engined Plus 8 to the range to provide a frightening machine which compared with nothing else, but still this product didn't dent Alfa Romeo's market position much either.

The Giulia 1600 Spider Duetto continued in production only until 1968, though the Giulia Spider 1300 Junior, a reversion to the engine size of the immensely successful Giulietta, employing the same body shell as the 1600, went on until 1972. It seems a little surprising that the smaller-engined version was only slower than the 1600 by 7mph (11kph), whilst reducing the Italian road tax by an appreciable lump. With estimated average fuel consumptions of 25mpg (11l/100km) for the 1600 and 28–30 (10–9l/100km) for the 1300, there was also a fair saving to be made from the smaller car's fuel costs. Therefore, the slight acceleration and top speed penalties were thought by many to be worth suffering for the privilege of owning an Alfa Romeo Spider.

With the 'Duetto' name tag being dropped

Specification – Alfa Romeo Spider Junior 1300

Model 1300 Spider Junior
Year 1968–74

Type 2-seat, sports roadster
Wheelbase 2,250mm
Track 1,324mm (F); 1,274mm (R)
Tyre sizes 155 × 15 all round
Brakes Disc on all four wheels
Suspension Helical coil springs all round, with unequal length transverse links and roll bar front, upper triangular link and lower struts rear
Engine 1,290cc twin ohc
No. of cylinders 4 in line
Bore/stroke 74mm × 75mm
Induction 2 horizontal twin-choke
Ignition Coil and distributor
Power output 89bhp @ 6,000rpm
Transmission 5-speed gearbox in unit with engine, driving rear wheels
Gear ratios 1st 15.033:1; 2nd 9.065:1; 3rd 6.149:1; 4th 4.555:1; 5th 3.917:1; reverse 13.712:1

Versions catalogued 1300 Spider Junior, Spider Junior 1.3 (1971–74)

---

for the 1968 season, Alfa Romeo now offered only two open two-seaters: the Giulia Spider 1300 Junior and the Spider 1750. The 1300 was introduced in 1968 as a supplement to the range and, for 1970, the 1750 came with improved suspension and the square-cut 'Kamm' rear end. The cleaner lines of the Kamm-tailed 1750 were to win through and so the Giulia Spider Junior 1300 inherited the line along with its larger relatives, as the expansion of the volume manufacture took place of the 1750 and newer 2000 Spiders.

The first series, round-tailed, Spider 1300 Junior, introduced in 1968.

This is the Kamm-tailed Spider 1300 Junior.

However, the re-introduction of the 1600-engined model in 1972 began with a run of 928 Giulia Spider 1600s before it was re-named the Spider Junior 1600. So the same fate as had befallen the Saloon and Coupe Alfa Romeo models in the Giulia range now came to the Spiders. They would, in future, be known only by the numbers which identified their respective engine sizes, with the tag 'Junior' added to the 1600 model.

THE 1750 SPIDER SERIES

Knocking over the challenge of Britain's Lotus Elan was achieved by the introduction, in 1967, of Alfa Romeo's 1750 Spider. Because the performance of the Giulia 1600 range of cars was beginning to fall behind in its market sector by 1967, Alfa Romeo enlarged the engine, refined the lines of the Giulia models and introduced their successor

as the 1750 Series, borrowing another name from the past. The 1750 Spider was only slightly changed on the outside, with a bumper insert across the radiator grille and the direction indicator repeater lights moved forward along the side-panel to a position ahead of the front wheels. An additional repeater was then fitted to each side panel at the rear of the rear wheels to improve visual safety when a car was approached obliquely.

Some 854 examples of this new model were built in that year, against 2,958 Spider 1600 Duettos during the same period. The Spider Junior 1300 was not yet on the market, so the competition for Alfa Romeo consisted only, at this stage, of the slightly larger-engined (and long-in-the-tooth) Lancia Flavia 1800 Convertible, the Fiat Spiders, nothing from Germany or France and then the British contingent. This last collection consisted of the MGB, the Triumph TR4 and the already mentioned Lotus. The Lotus was the only real challenge, as the other British offerings

The Spider 1750 round-tail, outside . . .

had single camshaft, pushrod valve gear engines, which were no match for Alfa Romeo.

Two specific versions of the 1750 were produced from 1968. Counting the right-hand-drive model, exported mainly to Great Britain, as a variant of the original European version, the other, with 'cleaned up' breathing, was specially built for the US market. This latter model was fitted with indirect fuel injection, using a mechanically operated Spica pump. In theory, both the European and North American models produced 118bhp and had a maximum speed of 115mph (185kph), with a 0–80mph (0–100kph) time of ten seconds.

By 1971, the next phase in the 1750 Spider's development arrived as the 2000 Series of cars also came on to the market.

This was a revamped Spider body, with a squared-off tail of the type conceived by Dr Kamm. With its cleaned-up body styling, recessed door handles and larger engine, the Alfa Romeo 1750 Spider not only looked less as though it had emerged from a jelly mould, but it sat on the road and performed better, too. The brake horsepower of the 1750, at 118, was a notable improvement of some nine horsepower over its predecessor, the 1600, with a corresponding improvement in road speed.

The 1750 Spider Veloce was available in the model years 1967 to 1971, with a very few USA models built in 1972, overlapping its successor for a year, in the true Alfa Romeo tradition of ensuring the reliability of a new model before killing off its predecessor. In that time, the 1750 sold well, representing

. . . and inside, showing the higher level of trim in the 1750.

Specification – Alfa Romeo 1750 Spider Veloce

Model 1750 Spider Veloce
Year 1967–71

Type 2-seat, 2-door roadster
Wheelbase 2,250mm
Track 1,324mm (F); 1,274mm (R)
Tyre sizes 165SR × 14 all round
Brakes Disc on all four wheels
Suspension Helical coil springs all
   round, with unequal length transverse
   links and anti-roll bar front, upper
   triangular link and lower struts rear
Engine 1,779cc twin ohc
No. of cylinders 4 in line
Bore/stroke 80mm × 88.5mm
Induction 2 horizontal twin-choke
Ignition Coil and distributor
Power output 118bhp @ 5,500rpm
Transmission 5-speed gearbox in unit
   with engine, driving rear wheels
Gear ratios
   *With 10/41 crown wheel and pionion
   (European Versions)* 1st 13.53:1; 2nd
   8.159:1; 3rd 5.535:1; 4th 4.1:1; 5th
   3.239:1; reverse 12.341:1
   *With 9/41 crown wheel and pinion (USA
   version)* 1st 15.033:1; 2nd 9.065:1; 3rd
   6.150:1; 4th 4.555:1; 5th 3.598:1;
   reverse 13.712:1;

Versions catalogued 1750 Spider
   Veloce Roadster

about six per cent of total production of all 1750 models, with some 8,723 Spiders leaving the line at Arese.

IN COMES THE SPIDER 2000

The Kamm-tailed body design on the Alfa Romeo Spider heralded the introduction of the 2000 version of this now well-established and very popular car. The engine was developed from the 1750, which in turn came from the 1600, but now an increase in the cylinder bore was the major change, to 84mm, leaving the stroke at 88.5mm, which made the resultant engine capacity some 1,962cc. This increase in engine size improved the power output by another 14bhp, making the 2000 a 132bhp engine.

Like the Kamm-tailed 1750, the 2000 had faired-in headlamps, aimed at improving the aerodynamics of the car, though the USA took a more cynical view of it, continuing to insist that headlamp fairings were not fitted to models exported into that market. The reason, it seems, was that the Americans were suspicious that condensation would form on the transparent fairings and distort the headlamp beams sufficiently to cause distress to other road users.

Despite American legislation leaning

Specification – Alfa Romeo 2000 Spider (post-1750)

Model 2000 Spider
Year 1971–82

Type 2-seat, 2-door roadster
Wheelbase 2,250mm
Track 1,324mm (F); 1,274mm (R)
Tyre sizes 165HR × 14 all round
Brakes Disc on all four wheels
Suspension Helical coil springs all
   round, with unequal length transverse
   links and anti-roll bar front, upper
   triangular link and lower struts rear
Engine 1,962cc twin ohc
No. of cylinders 4 in line
Bore/stroke 84mm × 88.5mm
Induction 2 horizontal twin-choke
Ignition Coil and distributor
Power output 133bhp @ 5,500rpm
   (1971–77), 128bhp @ 5,300rpm
   (1975–82)
Transmission 5-speed gearbox in unit
   with engine, driving rear wheels

Versions catalogued 2000 Spider
   Veloce, 2000 Spider Veloce (RHD),
   2000 Spider USA, Spider 2000
   (133bhp), Spider 2000 (128bhp)

heavily against the open sports car the Alfa Romeo Spider continued to sell moderately well in North America, where it was regarded with a certain special reverence saved in that vast continent for works of art which came from the Old World to the New. Indeed, a special model, now complying with the California State safety and environment legislation, was offered as the Spider 2.0 USA.

With just fourteen 1750 Spiders leaving Arese in 1972, and a further two in 1973 – no doubt assembled from parts which lay in the factory and almost certainly not routine production vehicles assembled on the line – the 2000 was well and truly in the market place by 1971, though only 823 examples were actually sold in that year. The year 1972 was, in fact, the best one for production figures of the Spider, these all being the standard European models, some in right-hand drive, but the vast majority being left-hand.

The best production year for that first version of the Spider 2000 was 1972, when 2,902 were built. Only 1,418 were built in 1973 and 1,002 in 1974, from where production diminished into three figures per

The 1975 Spider 2000.

The cockpit of the Spider 1300 Junior, showing it to be a thoroughly practical car.

year until the withdrawal of that particular version in 1977. In the meantime, a lower-powered version, of 128bhp, and environmentally clean, came along in 1975 to boost flagging sales. Some 770 of this newer version were produced in 1975, falling to 728 in the following year, then rising to over 1,000 for four consecutive years up to 1980, when production fell to 524 for 1981 and rose again to 1,581 in its final production year of 1982.

Imports of the Spider 2000 to Great Britain ceased in 1978, as a consequence of Alfa Romeo's decision to produce no more in right-hand drive form and arising from the drop in sales of this model, largely because it was only available in left-hand drive. Since that time, many have found their way into Britain by private import and have been converted to right-hand drive, all strictly against Alfa Romeo's warranty policy and advice.

THE SPIDER JUNIOR

Production of the Spider 1300 Junior began in 1968, with the round-tailed version which accompanied the period 1600. In 1970, with

the advent of the square-tailed versions of the two larger models, the Junior followed the same course. It was an immensely popular little car, as open sports cars went for the time, not least because it was of only 1,290cc engine capacity, but also because it represented tremendous value and fun for money.

The Spider 1300 Junior was essentially, as far as Alfa Romeo was concerned, a downmarket version of its open two-seater, dimensionally the same as the larger-engined car, but fitted with inexpensive pressed steel wheels, no headlamp fairings, only single, forward-located, direction indicator repeaters and, of course, the 1,290cc engine instead of the 1,750cc. The price difference between the 1300 Junior and the 2000 in 1972 was 660,000 Lire, the 2000 costing marginally under 32 per cent more than the Junior. This price differential seems also to have carried over into the British and North American markets.

The heart of the Spider Junior was its engine, the very component which no competitor could emulate. When you examine the various so-called sports cars which were on offer in Britain at the time, none came anywhere near the Alfa for

The Spiders (Junior, 1750, 2000, 1.6 & 2.0) and Their Adversaries

Car and Model	Engine Type and Size	Gearbox	Max. Speed		Consumption		GB Price
			mph	(kph)	mpg	(l/100km)	
Alfa Romeo 1750 Spider	1,779cc 4-cylinder twin ohc	5-speed	105	(170)	24–26	(12–11)	£2,270 (1970)
Lotus Elan Series 3 Roadster	1,598cc 4-cylinder twin ohc	5-speed	118	(190)	24–28	(12–10)	£2,010 (1970)
Fiat 124 Spider 1.8	1,756cc 4-cylinder twin ohc	5-speed	107	(172)	24–27	(12–10)	£1,700 (1972)
Sunbeam Alpine 1600 Roadster	1,592cc 4-cylinder pushrod ohv	4-speed	98	(158)	23–27	(12–10)	£ 878 (1970)
MGB 1800 Roadster	1,798cc 4-cylinder pushrod ohv	4-speed	104	(167)	21–24	(13–12)	£1,120 (1971)
Triumph TR4 Roadster	2,138cc 4-cylinder pushrod ohv	4-speed	109	(175)	24–26	(12–11)	£1,058 (1967)
Triumph TR5 Roadster	2,498cc 6-cylinder pushrod ohv	4-speed	117	(188)	20–24	(14–12)	£1,240 (1968)
Alfa Romeo Spider 1300 Junior	1,298cc 4-cylinder twin ohc	5-speed	103	(166)	29–31	(10–9)	£1,900 (1972)
Austin Healey Sprite Mk 2/MG Midget	1,198cc 4-cylinder pushrod ohv	4-speed	98	(158)	31–35	(9–8)	£ 905 (1970)
Triumph Spitfire Roadster	1,296cc 4-cylinder pushrod ohv	4-speed	95	(153)	30–32	(9)	£ 870 (1967)
Alfa Romeo 2000 Spider	1,962cc 4-cylinder twin ohc	5-speed	115	(185)	24–28	(12–10)	£2,439 (1971)
Triumph TR6 Roadster	2,498cc 6-cylinder pushrod ohv	5-speed	110	(175)	23–25	(12–11)	£1,334 (1969)
Jensen-Healey	1,973cc 4-cylinder twin ohc	5-seed	119	(191.5)	22–24	(13–12)	£1,810 (1976)
Triumph TR7 Roadster	1,998cc 4-cylinder single ohc	5-speed	114	(183)	24–28	(12–10)	£5,959 (1980)
Alfa Romeo Spider 2.0 (1990)	1,962cc 4-cylinder twin ohc	5-speed	118	(190)	24–30	(12–9)	£15,495 (1990)

specification, performance or sheer pleasure, though it *is* fair to say that they didn't come near the Spider Junior for price either. The badge-engineered MG Midget and Austin Healey Sprite clones of each other were equipped with the gutsy little BMC 'A' Series engine, a single-camshaft pushrod overhead valve unit with two carburettors, a cast iron cylinder block and far less power. The Triumph Spitfire was a similar story, using a developed version of the old Standard Ten engine, again a two-carburettor, single-cam pushrod overhead valve unit. All three of these makes carried illustrious names, which had earlier left their marks on history, but none of their current offerings measured up to their epic namesakes. On the other hand, the Alfa Romeo Giulia Spider 1300 Junior *did* measure up to its predecessor and shone above its adversaries.

With its position confirmed in the market, the Spider Junior 1300, as the direct successor to the Giulietta Spider, was joined in 1972 by another Spider Junior, this time the 1600. It was again a case of history repeating itself, except that in this case, the only physical feature which changed between the 1300 and the 1600 was the engine. For 1972 only, the 1600 was referred to as the Giulia

Specification – Alfa Romeo Spider 1300/1600 Junior Spider

Model Spider Junior
Year 1974–81

Type 2-seat sports roadster
Wheelbase 2,250mm
Track 1,324mm (F); 1,274mm (R)
Tyre sizes 155 × 15 all round
Brakes Disc on all four wheels
Suspension All-helical coil springs with unequal length transverse links and anti-roll bar front, triangular upper link and lower struts rear
Engine 1,290cc/1,570cc dohc
No. of cylinders 4 in line
Bore/stroke 74mm × 75mm/ 78mm × 82mm
Induction 2 horizontal twin-choke
Ignition Coil and distributor
Power output 1300: 89bhp @ 6,000rpm; 1600: 108bhp @ 5,600rpm
Transmission 5-speed gearbox in unit with engine, driving rear wheels
Gear ratios 1st 15.033:1; 2nd 8.159:1; 3rd 6.149:1; 4th 4.10:1; 5th 3.917:1; reverse 13.712:1

Versions catalogued Spider 1300 Junior, Spider 1600 Junior (109bhp), Spider 1600 Junior (102bhp)

1600, thereafter being labelled Spider Junior 1600. All the trim and body features which helped to keep the price of the Junior sufficiently below that of the Spider 2000 remained intact, with no attempt to improve them and increase cost.

The new Spider Junior restored a direct challenge to the Lotus Elan, except for price, of course, since the Alfa Romeo was somewhat more expensive. The price argument supporting the differential between the two included such considerations as the all-alloy Alfa engine versus the cheaper modified Ford unit in the Lotus, the all-steel body unit of the Alfa Romeo against the glassfibre body

The 1974 version of the 1600 Spider.

of the Lotus and, of course, charisma. Whether it was liked or not, the *image* of driving an Alfa Romeo was more acceptable than that of driving a Lotus, because one was perceived as being further upmarket than the other, despite the Lotus having excellent all-round performance.

1300 VERSUS 1600 SPIDERS

There was mixed opinion among the press pundits about the merits of the Giulia Spider 1300 Junior as an alternative to the slightly

In 1974, using the Alfetta floorpan and running gear, Pininfarina produced a design exercise known as the 'Eagle'. This is the second (1975) version which could have gone into production, but . . .

The Spider 2.0 USA of 1978, note the larger bumpers.

larger-engined 1600. But there was no denying that it had a place in the market, if only to provide a quality example of engineering against which to measure some of the quite appalling open two-seaters offered by other manufacturers in the guise of 'sports car'.

As has already been said, the 1600 had better general performance than the 1300 and had slightly better roadholding, simply because there was more rubber on the road through its larger tyres and because it had more torque to help drag the car out of difficult spots. In driving the 1600, snap gear changes were not quite so important to achieve given manoeuvres, and so it was a slightly more forgiving car to handle.

Both models were equipped with the five-speed all-synchromesh gearbox and their trim and finish, inside and out, were much the same, too. Price was the principal remaining difference between the two models. There was around 400,000 Lire between the two during 1972, when the 1300 was in demise and the 1600 was returning to production. Hard-tops were now available for both, but were some way from being offered as part of the standard specification, as in more modern times.

The continuing justification for manufacturing the Spider Junior 1300 returns to the subject of fuel costs and road taxes of cars in Italy and other parts of Europe. Alfa Romeo rightly held the view that if you could actually capture your market early enough, then you had a fair chance of retaining a large part of it. So there was an incentive to create the best possible conditions for Alfa ownership by producing a car young, not-so-rich enthusiasts could afford to buy *and* run.

Alfa Romeo had learned from the early days of the Giulietta that they could ask a price for a product and that people would pay that price if they saw it as reasonable. The problem was to ensure that after they had bought it, they could afford the vehicle road

taxes and enjoy low fuel consumption, so as to be able to run the car for no higher costs than a contemporary small family car. The Spider 1300 filled this gap admirably, whilst the 1600 continued to offer reasonable economy and higher performance, without going the whole hog and buying the 2000.

The last Spider 1300 Junior left Arese in 1978, the only 1300 produced in that year, after a total production run of 7,238 cars. Including the Giulia 1600 Spiders produced in 1972, the total production run of Spider Junior 1600s was 4,848 when the model was discontinued in 1981. Two versions of the 1600 Junior were produced in that time, the first version with a 109bhp power output, the later, cleaner, version producing only 102bhp and built alongside the 109bhp version for two years, in 1974 and 1975.

ARRIVAL OF THE SPIDER 2.0 SERIES

It was in 1974 that the term '2.0' first came into use on the Alfa Romeo Spider, ultimately to replace '2000' as the definition of engine size. The first 2.0 was in fact an export model, the Spider 2.0 USA, though the new definition, which was a pan-European agreement between the major manufacturers, was not yet applied to the rest of the Alfa Romeo range universally, but progressively as a new variant came into production. For example, there were other models in the Alfa Romeo range where some were referred to under the old system, for example the Alfetta GTV 2000 and the Alfetta Saloon 1.6, to quote a case. And even then, Alfa Romeo itself appears not to have been consistent, since there were Spider models built and referred to by Arese as '2000' some time after the first use of '2.0'.

The Spider 2000 continued in production in 132bhp form until 1977, with the 'Euro-clean' 128bhp engine building up production numbers from 1975. It is quite interesting

Specification – Alfa Romeo Spider 1.6/2.0

Model Spider 1.6/2.0
Year 1982–90

Type 2-seat, 2-door roadster
Wheelbase 2,250mm
Track 1,324mm (F); 1,274mm (R)
Tyre sizes 1.6: 165R-14-84H; 2.0: 185/70HR-14
Brakes Disc on all four wheels
Suspension Helical coil springs all round, with unequal length transverse links and anti-roll bar front, upper triangular link, lower struts and stabilizer bar rear
Engine Two sizes: 1,570cc and 1,962c twin ohc
No. of cylinders 4
Bore/stroke 78mm × 82mm/ 84mm × 88.5mm
Induction 2 horizontal twin-choke
Ignition Coil and distributor
Power output 1.6: 104bhp @ 5,500rpm; 2.0: 128bhp @ 5,400rpm
Transmission 5-speed gearbox in unit with engine, driving rear wheels
Gear ratios 1st 13.546:1; 2nd 8.150:1; 3rd 5.555:1; 4th 4.10:1; 5th 3.243:1; reverse 12.341:1

Versions catalogued 1.6 Spider, 2.0 Spider, 2.0 Spider USA, 2.0 Spider Veloce USA, 2.0 Spider Quadrifoglio Verde, 2.0 Spider Quadrifoglio Verde USA

now to reflect on the phasing of popularity of open two-seat sports cars, by examining the production figures of the Spider 2000 and 2.0 year-on-year from its inception. In 1971, the Spider 2000's first year, 838 were built, increasing to almost 2,000 in 1972, falling back in 1973, then sticking around the 1,200 volume for the next three years. Numbers dropped a little in 1978, rose again in 1979 and peaked in 1980, falling back again, now to only 207, for 1982. Spider USAs, on the other hand, were produced in consistently larger numbers between 1973 and 1979, the largest annual volume of that model being 3,242 cars in 1974.

The year 1974 is a notable year in the production career of the 2-litre Spider for another reason, too. That was the year in which the Spider story could easily have taken a different direction, by the introduction of an Alfetta-based open two-seater, designed by Pininfarina and called the 'Alfetta Spyder Eagle' (Pininfarina preferring to spell 'Spyder' with a 'Y'). An initial design exercise was produced in 1972, on the heels of the announcement of the Alfetta Saloon and before the Alfetta GT appeared on the scene. However, that early project was still-born, but in 1974 was revived as the 'Eagle', a rather slab-like two-seater with detachable transparent top and integral roll-over bar which also formed the rear quarter panel. Another, more avant-garde Eagle arrived in 1975, but by that time, Alfa Romeo had decided to stick with the Spider they knew.

Styling changes to the Alfa Spider were few after 1980, with minor cosmetic variations making up most of them. However, front-end styling had already begun to be influenced by American safety standards, with the front bumper coming in for particular attention as the result of demands for minimum impact yield capacity. On the 1978 example of the Spider 2.0 USA, the radiator grille almost disappeared behind the moulded front bumper, with the result that the Alfa Romeo badge found its way on to the centre of the bumper instead of on the radiator grille, where it would never have been seen. The direction indicator side repeaters were also enlarged from the small, round button type to a flat, rectangular example on that model.

Introducing a front air dam in 1983, the Spider of that year also featured a new variation on the safe front bumper theme. Using a slight modification of the original body pressings, Alfa Romeo had managed to make the front end look quite different,

A full frontal of the 1982 Spider 2.0.

The 1983 Spider 2.0 featured a black plastic add-on rear spoiler and US-style bumpers.

This is the 1986 version of the Spider 2.0
Quadrifoglio Verde . . . and inset is
the inside of the same car.

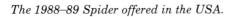

The 1988–89 Spider offered in the USA.

simply by creating a moulded plastic radiator grille of uncharacteristic, almost triangular shape, located in the centre and forming part of the front bumper. With trim cappings over the two main bumper sections, the radiator grille was made to stand out and at least be noticed, so that the car could be identified by its radiator once more. The 1986 model's introduction also saw the use of side-skirts and a quite ugly black plastic rear spoiler, the moulding of which wrapped round the tail of the car to meet with the oversize rear bumper, also plastic.

This variant of the Spider continued in production right up to 1990, being offered in three versions: the Spider 1.6, the Spider 2.0 and the Spider 2.0 Quadrifoglio Verde. Of the two 2-litre variants, one came with the side-skirts and the other did not. Interior detail, engine and gearbox were identical between the two cars, whilst the only difference between the 1.6 and the basic form of 2.0 was the engine size. The Spider suffered from low sales for quite a while, then when the US market warmed up again and flexed to accommodate the import of open cars again, the Spider's sales revived, with the result that an entirely new version was launched in 1990.

THE SPIDER OF TODAY

In June 1990, Alfa Romeo announced that it was to launch its new Spider into the British market, to be available again after a lapse of twelve years. This was truly exciting news to that small, but committed, group of Alfa enthusiasts who had bought other makes of cars or had embarked upon the tortuous route of the personal imports system to bring a car into Britain. The total sales potential for the Spider in Britain is probably only a couple of hundred a year, but the charisma from that is considered by Alfa Romeo (Great Britain) Limited to be worth the trouble. The only problem in Britain is that the cars

---

Specification – Alfa Romeo Spider 1.6/2.0 (1990 Series)

Model Spider 1.6/2.0
Year 1990–on

Type 2-seat, 2-door roadster
Wheelbase 2,250mm
Track 1,324mm (F); 1,274mm (R)
Tyre sizes 1.6: 175/60HR-15; 2.0: 195/60HR-15
Brakes Disc on all four wheels
Suspension Helical coil springs all round, with unequal length transverse links and anti-roll bar front, upper triangular link, lower struts and stabilizer bar rear
Engine Two sizes: 1,570cc and 1,962cc twin ohc
No. of cylinders 4
Bore/stroke 78mm × 82mm/ 84mm × 88.5mm
Induction 2 horizontal twin-choke
Ignition Coil and distributor
Power output 1.6: 104bhp @ 5,500rpm; 2.0: 120bhp @ 5,800rpm
Transmission 5-speed gearbox in unit with engine, driving rear wheels
Gear ratios 1st 13.546:1; 2nd 8.150:1; 3rd 5.555:1; 4th 4.10:1; 5th 3.243:1; reverse 12.341:1

Versions catalogued 1.6 Spider, 2.0 Spider, 2.0 Spider USA

---

offered are available only in left-hand drive. However, the broader market potential is probably more than 5,000 a year.

Whatever the sales potential, Alfa Romeo has clearly seen the Spider as a continuing benefit to their total sales plan, so it has remained, to become as much of an institution in today's motoring world as the Morgan is in Great Britain. Today's Spider has a softer, rounder look, yet retains all the classic elegance of the original lines. Gone are the sharp-edged and ugly items of black trim, to be replaced with gently curved and shaped items, colour-matched to the car's own body colour. The bumpers remain of a plastic material with limited yield characteristics, but they are now the same colour as the bodywork, as are the door mirror casings.

The longer side panels contain a new side repeater for the direction indicators, which blends in more smoothly. The front bumper looks as though it was designed for the car and not stuck on as an afterthought. The radiator grille is within the bumper, but now has a shape similar to all the other current Alfa Romeo models, with the badge where it should be, within that grille. The rear light cluster looks like other cars in the Alfa Romeo family and the sharp edge to the tail is replaced by a smoothly contoured rear deck which again emphasizes the softer line of the 1990s. This is a car of which Carrozzeria Pininfarina can truly be proud, since it has all the features of a thoroughly modern two-seater, combined with the identity of a car which is twenty-five years old.

Inside, the Spider remains much as it has always been, with leather-like vinyl upholstery, though hide seating is available, a simulated suede covering to the centre console and deep-pile carpets with footmats. The instruments are much the same as on the previous version, whilst screen and face-level vents are fitted into the dash for heating, ventilation and de-misting. Completing the interior specification are electrically-operated side windows and door mirrors, speed-sensitive power steering, a stereo radio-cassette player, as well as lockable fuel filler and bootlid release catches. On the outside, a heavy-duty, one-man operated canvas hood is fitted, though a removable hard-top is also supplied with the car. Alloy road wheels complete the detail specification, fitted with low-profile tyres of 195/60R 15 size to both 1.6 and 2.0 versions of the car.

A SPIDER ON THE ROAD

Much has been said in the motoring press about the merits of classic Alfas and their prices *vis-à-vis* other classic sports cars. In Great Britain, the main classic competition consists of the Triumph TRs 2 to 6, the MGA and MGB, the Lotus Elan Roadster and perhaps the TVR roadsters. The Morgan Plus Four is a particular cult car and doesn't really clash with the Alfa Spider. A really decent example of any of these cars will cost today around the same as a classic Alfa and the price of all of them is not far away from (in fact they could be slightly more than) the price today of a new Alfa Spider. The conclusion therefore is: why bother with an old car, when you *know* that a new example will cost around the same money, will be better protected against rust and can be kept in better condition because you *know* what it was like when you bought it? A brand new classic has a lot to recommend it.

Road tests emerging on the new Spider 2.0 describe it as a sheer delight, as a car of which the manufacturers have managed to retain its fascinating character. Handling is said still to be outstanding, improved by the modern additions of speed-sensitive power steering at the front and a limited-slip differential at the rear. Even with the old-fashioned concept of front engine and rear-wheel drive, this car corners superbly with power on and without rolling the occupants across the passenger compartment.

It has been suggested that the only way to unstick the Spider is to stuff it hard into a corner and then lift off – but even then, the car thinks twice about oversteering, though its suspension doesn't exactly like rough surfaces. But then, it *is* a living classic. But what a car it would be with the 2.0 Twin Spark engine. The Spider's 10.2-second 0–60mph (0–100kph) time would *really* come down then, and its general performance would significantly improve, with the benefit of an extra 28bhp. Whatever the future holds for the Spider is in the development stage, for its successor is expected in 1993.

10 From Alfasud to 33

THE STRUGGLE FOR SURVIVAL

As the decade of the 1970s drew to its close, Alfa Romeo was compelled to look at its performance in world markets and re-appraise its position. Having been involved, down the years, in manufacturing electricity generators, agricultural tractors, railway locomotives, road rollers, aero engines, trucks and buses, as well as cars, it was now feeling the pinch. Meanwhile Finmeccanica, the arm of Instituto Ricostruzione Industriale which was responsible for the funding and overseeing the management of the state-owned engineering companies, was looking closely at its return on investment.

Already, as part of a process embarked upon to rationalize its operating costs. Alfa Romeo had withdrawn from many of its peripheral activities, leaving it only in the businesses of car manufacture, light buses and aero engines. Alfa Avio had established a niche in the licence manufacture of a number of aero engines, as well as the reconditioning of engines made by the leading international manufacturers, such as General Electric, Pratt and Whitney and Rolls-Royce, so was a very profitable unit.

Next on Alfa Romeo's agenda was an investigation into the viability of co-sourcing certain mechanical components with other Italian vehicle makers, such as Lancia and Fiat. There proved to be too little scope for further sharing of parts-bins of brake components, ignition and electrical parts, as many were already virtually common between manufacturers anyway, though the prospect of single-sourcing through one procurement centre, Fiat, was also investi-

gated. None of this brought sufficient savings to recover the costs of operating the plant at Pomigliano d'Arco, where the Alfasud variants were made, so Alfa Romeo's board of directors was forced to contemplate the need for a new model to recover flagging sales.

The 1970s had been a decade in which market fluctuations had been extreme. The 1973 international oil crisis had stopped industrial growth in its tracks, hitting the world's motor industry hardest. Stumbling growth had come in the mid-1970s, only to be dealt another body blow in 1979 with a further explosion in oil prices, whilst the inexorable growth of car imports from the Orient seemed unstoppable. Manufacturing and tooling costs were now at a peak and this was no time, in ordinary circumstances, for a car maker to be examining the prospect of developing a new range. But these were not ordinary times. Alfa Romeo had serious problems it was compelled to address, and so it began to seek more far-reaching solutions.

ANALYSING THE PROBLEM

The fundamental problem for Alfa Romeo now was survival in a market place suffering from gross over-supply. The Alfasud had filled its ideological objective admirably, having successfully filled the market niche occupied some years before by the Giulietta, and it had restored Alfa Romeo's place in the top end of the small family car market. But it had also encountered many problems which had impaired its potential commercial success.

The early production control and quality

problems are already well documented, but there were many other aspects to the predicament in which Alfa Romeo found itself by the dawn of the 1980s. The sheer cost now of acquiring new press tools for body panels was too high to allow for any mistakes, yet Alfasud sales were in decline and there was nowhere else to go but produce a successor. That successor, however, had to avoid the quality problems, the corrosion, the rear body strength problem which had inhibited the creation of a hatchback version and the warranty costs on the Alfasud.

As a consequence of all these difficulties, the Alfa Romeo dealer network was weak outside Italy. This brought its own set of problems, in that many dealers were perhaps not as committed as they might have been, so reducing the quality of service support given to customers. The result of all these deliberations was a decision to meet the oriental problem head-on and go out to talk to the Japanese competitors on equal terms, with a view to establishing the kind of co-operative deal which Leyland in Great Britain had struck with Honda.

ARNA IS BORN

A new model was essential to Alfa Romeo in the small family saloon class, partly to give them a chance to wipe the slate clean with regard to their own past problems and partly to give the market place sufficient confidence for the company to restructure the dealer network where it was weak. The whole idea of a co-operative deal with a Japanese car manufacturer was to produce a new model in less than normal development time, with less than normal development and tooling costs. The advantage of going to any Japanese maker was the volume capacity and cost-saving in the supply of components, added to which most Japanese manufacturers had, through the 1970s, licked any quality problems they might have had.

The five-door Arna SL.

The Japanese manufacturer which married up with Alfa Romeo was Nissan and the car to be produced as a result of the deal was a version of the new Nissan 'Cherry' to be known as the 'Arna' ('A'lfa 'R'omeo-'N'issan 'A'uto) under the Alfa Romeo badge and as the 'Cherry Europe' with a Nissan badge.

The year 1983 saw the final demise of the Alfasud Saloon and the release of the Arna 1.2L and SL models. The new model was to be built in both badged versions at Pomigliano d'Arco, the old Alfasud factory, and at a new plant at Pratola Serra, near Avellino, some

The Arna 3-door 1.5TI. This was to be the sporty version of the Arna, but it didn't quite match its predecessor's performance.

30 miles east of Naples. Press tool modifications for the Arna and Cherry Europe were made relatively easily and the Japanese original body unit seemed to present no major problems in the process of 'cloning' it to accept the Alfasud mechnical components. The latter consisted of the flat-four engine with the Alfasud longitudinal gearbox unit together with the front suspension and braking assemblies. The rear suspension remained Nissan Cherry, whilst the interior was very much improved Nissan to make it more acceptable to discerning Alfa buyers.

First conceived in 1981, as the basis of the co-operative agreement between the two companies, the Arna/Cherry Europe project was to be built from body panels imported from Japan in the newly built robot-equipped Avellino factory. These body units would then be transported in containers to Pomigliano d'Arco, where complete cars, badged Nissan or Alfa Romeo, would be assembled alongside each other. The objective was to build up to a production level of 60,000 cars a year by 1986. It was seen as an exciting time. On the one hand, Nissan were using the design as the new Cherry in Japan and elsewhere in the world – their product unit cost helped down by the association – whilst on the other, a new air of respectability was lent to Japanese cars in Italy.

THE DREAM FAILS

Broadly similar in size to its noted predecessor, from a driver's point of view, the Arna never had quite the same 'feel'. The Nissan-designed rear suspension seemed not to allow the car to handle in quite the same way as the Alfasud and it didn't seem quite so crisp. The all-up weight wasn't that much different from the Alfasud and weight distribution was also similar. Some private individuals did try stiffening up the rear end

and that did have an improving effect on the handling of the car, but in all theoretical respects, it should have been the equal of the Alfasud, with its drag co-efficient of 0.38 and the stringent efforts put in by the Alfa Romeo engineering team, led by Filippo Surace.

With its higher level of trim and fittings than the corresponding Alfasud model it succeeded, the Arna still was not a commercial success. Despite the most careful market research, indicating the need for a slightly upmarket successor to the Alfasud at a comparable price – all of which the Arna was – the new model proved to be a sales disaster. First failing to reach volume production targets, when the Arna did begin to emerge from Avellino in quantity, the showrooms just filled up with unsold stocks. By 1986, they were being sold off for almost as little as customers wanted to pay for them. The same fate befell the Nissan Cherry Europe and by 1987 the two models had been discontinued.

From whatever perspective we examine the Arna today, in hindsight, it should have met a better level of success then it did. A great deal of effort had gone into its adaptation from the Japanese original design. The modification of the floorpan had been given far closer attention by Surace's team than many an original Alfa Romeo chassis design; the metal used in its pressed panelwork was carefully selected with northern European markets in mind, where damp weather and liberal use of salt on winter roads were a perennial nightmare for any car designer. Even the seat bases, imported from Japan, were covered in Italy to Italian designs and taste. Perhaps the keys to the Arna's failure to capture the imagination of those who had bought its predecessor in quantity were simply its shape and origin. The one major thing which it was not appears to have been the one thing which precluded its sale in large quantities – Italian.

ENTER A NEW ALFA 33

Filippo Surace's other major contribution to Alfa Romeo's product range *was* a success, however, and it was the car which was destined to take over the role of successor to the Alfasud. Conceived at around the same time as the Arna, but aimed a step up from that model, this was the Alfa Romeo 33. Taking the name from a distinguished racing model to give a little extra charisma was not new to Alfa Romeo. They had already done it successfully with the earlier '1750' and 'Alfetta' models, so it was seen as appropriate and opportune to take another great racing name and use it to name a new

car and raise their product out of the marketing doldrums.

So it was that in a flurry of publicity a new model was announced in 1983, called the Alfa 33. The first press releases were issued with a picture of the new car standing adjacent to a T33 sports-racing car of the type which had, in 1975 and 1977, won the World Championship of Makes for Alfa Romeo. Developed from the Alfasud, but positively a larger car, the new model used many components from its antecedent and the first version to be released was the 1.3 model, which was quickly joined by a 1.5 variant. Once again, it was a case of releasing a new model in a low-powered form, to allow

As usual, Italian police forces used Alfa Romeos and here are city police Alfa 33s posing for the camera.

The engine compartment of the Arna leaves no doubt of the car's heritage.

improvement of performance to follow in the next stage.

The 33 was, and is, a five-door hatchback. It was designed to look something like an orthodox three-box saloon car with the distinct advantage of a large rear access aperture for those people who had the need of a hatchback, but wanted the appearance of a sporty saloon, albeit with a somewhat shorter rear end than conventional. The lesson of the Alfasud had been learned soundly and taken on board. The result was a roomy car with a much stronger rear structure and all the advantages of styling and material development which had come along in the eleven years since the Alfasud was first announced to the market place.

One glance at the engine compartment of the Alfa 33 told the world at large the heritage of this new Alfa Romeo, a car which began to re-establish the company's reputation for interesting and exciting family vehicles. But before the year was out, an entirely new version of the 33 was to be released which was totally unexpected. This new model featured an adventurous development of the original Alfasud engine/drivetrain concept, in that it was a four-wheel drive. In simple terms, with the advantage of the longitudinally placed engine and gearbox of the front-wheel drive original, it was easy to extend an output shaft from the gearbox and provide drive to the rear wheels. The new car was called the 'Alfa 33 4 × 4' and was fitted with the 1,490cc engine.

With a higher level of interior trim and fittings than its two front-wheel-drive siblings, the 4 × 4/4 × 2 drive split, which was operated by a lever positioned just ahead of the normal five-speed gear lever. Four-wheel drive had become a fashion at that time and no self-respecting sporty motorist who could afford it was without a 4 × 4. Alfa Romeo therefore seized their chance of releasing a model which was just a little roomier than Germany's Audi 80 4 × 4, a chunk less expensive and which carried the name of a car maker which had an enviable reputation for sporting cars in Europe.

By 1984, following again the example of the Alfasud (and again incorporating the lessons learned from that model), a new station wagon was released, eventually to be built in two versions of the Alfa 33. The 'Sportwagon 33', by its name, clearly and unashamedly declared its position to prospective owners and in 4 × 4 form was aimed at carving out a new niche for Alfa Romeo in the market place. However, the 4 × 4 variant did not sell well enough to justify the volumes envisaged, so was dropped by the end of 1985, though the station wagon remained in production as a popular version of the 33.

DEVELOPMENT AND CONSOLIDATION

Work continued on the development of the flat-four Alfa Romeo 'Boxer' engine and the *Quadrifoglio Verde* – the Green Cloverleaf – version was top of the range for a couple of years. Then, in 1986, at about the time the company realized that the Arna had to go, a new version of the 33 engine was announced. So it wasn't *all* doom and gloom at Alfa Romeo, though the financial position of the company was beginning to show itself as pretty desperate. The new engine, though, lifted spirits for a time, since it *was* a pretty exciting release. This was the 1,712cc version of the 'Boxer' unit, to be known as the 1.7 model.

Power output of the new engine was 118bhp, whilst its torque rating was 108lb/ft, a notable improvement in performance potential from the smaller 1.5 version. As the Arna was being quietly phased out, the Alfa 33 Cloverleaf 1.7 was released, with a maximum speed of 122mph (196kph) and

Another saloon with an illustrious name was the Alfa 33, here shown in its first form of 1983.

handling remarkably close to the long popular Alfasud, At the same time, it will be remembered, the Sprint Coupe continued alongside the 33, so providing a direct link with the Alfasud and another platform for promoting the 1.7 engine – thus helping to spread the development cost.

With the demise of the 4 × 4 version of the Alfa 33, the product range consolidated for 1987 on two engine sizes and two body types. There was the 1.5TI version of the 33 Saloon, accompanied by the 1.5 Veloce, both powered by the now-familiar 1,490cc twin-carburettor engine. The 1.7 models, using the 1,712cc engine, consisted of the 1.7 Cloverleaf and

The new Alfa 33 in cutaway, showing its comfortable concept and rugged construction.

The 1.5 engined 4 x 4 Alfa 33 goes through its paces.

the 1.7 Veloce Saloons, accompanied by the 1.7 Sportwagon and the 1.7 Sportwagon Veloce. The Veloce versions of both Saloon and Sportwagon models were fitted with body styling kits, featuring front and rear spoilers as well as side-skirts to the bottom sills. Quoted performance figures for both

This was the new 1.7-litre Boxer engine introduced in 1986.

variants suggest that the styling kits were no more than that, though the front air dam has certainly, at higher road speeds than permitted in Great Britain, proved to help front-end stability by reducing lift.

However, despite all the effort put into the range of cars, with new models developed and improved, combined with the stringent review of manufacturing techniques and component utilization, Alfa Romeo still made losses. Finally, those losses were seen as far too great to be allowed to continue and the government stepped in to take its own remedial action.

UP FOR GRABS

In the autumn of 1986, partly as the consequence of Alfa Romeo's disastrous trading results, partly because there was a feeling in Italian political circles that the State should divest itself of some of its industrial holdings, and partly because there was a perceived gross over-supply in the European car market, the Italian government announced the decision that Finmeccanica, under government direction, was to offer the automotive division of Alfa Romeo for sale. Alfa Avio was to be incorporated into Aeritalia and the vehicle business sold to the highest bidder allowing, of course, for the best interests of Italy and its industry base.

There were two bidders for Alfa Romeo, both predictable: Ford and Fiat. It seemed clear from the outset that Ford's principal interest was caused by its own poor penetration of the Italian market, whilst it was being said in certain quarters that Fiat's interest was largely defensive and aimed at staving off a Ford invasion. The basic fact of the deal was that Ford offered initially to take 20 per cent of Alfa Romeo, increasing its stake to 51 per cent or more over three years, assuming responsibility for Alfa Romeo's massive debt after the first year, in ratio to its stake in the company.

Fiat's bid was seen by many in the money markets as being a counter to Ford, which set out to take 51 per cent of Alfa Romeo from the outset and assume management responsibility for Alfa's debts in full, subject to a restructuring of its financial position. Fiat proposed to merge Alfa Romeo with Lancia, moving some of the Lancia product into Arese to maximize that plant's production potential. A positive commitment was given to continue the Alfa Romeo name and product, though it was clear that some 'in-breeding' would take place between Alfa Romeo and other Fiat products.

In October 1986, Donald Petersen, Chairman of Ford Motor Company, visited Rome to meet the Italian Prime Minister, Bettino Craxi, and some of his ministers, in order to try to manoeuvre the deal towards Ford. However, the body of Italian political opinion regarded the American offer as a threat to the stability of Italy's motor industry and moved swiftly in favour of the Fiat bid, which was not only Italian and stronger than Ford's bid, but also considered as the base from which Fiat could take on the might of

Daimler Benz in Europe. Add to this the commitment from Cesare Romiti, Group Managing Director of Fiat, to renew the whole model range by 1990, and the public had a pretty convincing argument for the acceptance of Fiat's offer, which was approved by the government before the end of the year.

LIFE AFTER FIAT

Notwithstanding Signor Romiti's promise, apart from minor cosmetic changes, the Alfa 33 continued in production through 1989 and the first half of 1990 undisturbed, and seemingly sold quite well. Market statistics for sales in Great Britain showed a distinct return of confidence in Alfa Romeo products, no doubt partly enhanced by the improvement in quality stemming from Fiat's investment in the manufacturing company, but equally certainly by the improvement in sales support and dealer representation. Alfa Romeo dealers have been 'sorted out' several times over the last few years, leading to a feeling of insecurity on the part of owners and customers. The consequence of this had previously caused a decline in new car sales, but things have changed and are changing for the better, with the result that Alfa Romeo's star is rising in Britain and elsewhere in Europe.

June 1990 saw a major revamp of the Alfa 33. Now, if you consider Signor Romiti's 1986 promise of 'renewal' to be one of 'making new' rather than one of 'replacing', his promise has been fulfilled, for the 1990 Alfa 33, along with all the other model changes introduced in that year, was certainly a 'renewal'. Recognizable as a development of the 33, this new version was a revelation in many ways. It revealed a remarkable degree of attention paid to market research in the styling changes made, as it was now softer and of cleaner lines. The interior was extensively face-lifted, whilst on the outside, the radiator grille was changed, colour co-ordinated door mirrors were fitted in place of black, the door handles were improved and the rear end of the car was cleaned up and fitted with a much neater tail light cluster. But the real change was in the power house.

THE QUAD-CAM BOXER ENGINE

Back in April 1988, Alfa Romeo announced at the Turin Motor Show that it was to produce a four-cam version of the 'Boxer' engine. This engine was to be different in many ways, not least in its 'breathing'. Retaining the thimble tappet and shim

system of valve operation and adjustment, with two camshafts per bank of cylinders, the new engine had four valves per cylinder. But that wasn't all, since the four valves in each cylinder were timed in pairs, so allowing much finer phasing of induction and exhaust gases. The engine actually embodied four separate throttles, one to each induction passage on each cylinder bank and the fuel injectors were offset, so as to provide a larger volume of the fuel to the inlet valve with the lower overlap value.

Combining all these design developments with an integrated digital electronic fuel management system meant that Alfa Romeo had provided an engine with substantially improved brake horsepower and torque

The 1986 Alfa 33 Cloverleaf Saloon.

An Alfa 33 for the 1990s, the Quad-cam engined 33 Boxer 16V...

...and inside the engine of the Quad-cam Boxer.

throughout the band of operating speeds, so significantly improving overall performance of the vehicle into which it was to be fitted. In addition to that, the engine was endowed with improved fuel consumption, a cleaner exhaust resulting from more complete combustion and better engine idling. It was this engine which appeared in June 1990 to power the Alfa 33 Boxer 16V, flagship of the 33 range.

THE ALFA 33 FOR THE 1990s

As the quad-cam engine is the top-of-the-range model of Alfa 33, the word 'Boxer' was now incorporated into the car's title. ('Boxer' has become a fashionable word to use to describe an engine with horizontally opposed

Then there's the 33S Boxer 16V Permanent 4.

cylinders, ever since Ferrari adopted it as part of the name for its 512BB coupe.) So, on the back of the quad-cam engined Alfa 33 now appears the name '33 Boxer 16V'. Retaining the 87mm bore and 72mm stroke of the original 1,712cc engine and the 9.5:1 compression ratio, the quad-cam produces 137bhp at 6,500rpm, whereas the original two-cam (one per bank) engine now yields 110bhp at 5,800rpm.

The fuel injection system used on the quad-cam engine in the Alfa 33 is the Bosch ML4.1 injection and management system. On the fuel-injected original two-cam version of the engine, the Bosch L3.1 Jetronic fuel injection system combines with Bosch EZ10 digital ignition to provide the 'fire'. Gearing is the same for both 1990 versions of the 33, with a 3.320:1 top gear ratio giving 19.8mph (31.8kph) per 1,000 engine revolutions from a five-speed synchromesh gearbox. It doesn't take much arithmetic to realize that at 129mph (207.5kph), the engine revolutions amount to 6,500, which is a pretty high engine speed, though one rarely likely to be reached in top gear on many of Europe's roads. Fuel consumption, on the other hand, is somewhat better than the earlier Alfa 33s or Alfasuds, since 27.2mpg (10.4l/100km) is estimated for the quad-cam, according to the calculations resulting from the rather odd British Government ordained test system, whilst almost 36mpg (7.8l/100km) is said to be possible at 75mph (120kph) (not forgetting that Britain's statutory maximum speed limit is 70!).

For the first time on a small car, in Alfa Romeo terms, power steering was introduced, to ease the heavy low-speed steering characteristic of these front-wheel-drive cars and make them easy to manoeuvre in tight spots. It was a low-pressure speed-sensitive system, so that at high speeds there was no power assistance, because it wasn't needed. The result was that the steering on the 33s felt much the same at whatever speed the car was travelling.

As if those two new models weren't enough for the market at which the 33 is aimed, the turn of the decade 1990/91 brought news of three additions to the 33 range. The first, and perhaps most logical, was the revival of the 33 Sportwagon in the form of the '33 Sportwagon B.16V', accompanied by the quite odd revelation of a new 4 × 4 Sportwagon. That the 4 × 4 should return to the product range of Alfa Romeo is not the odd feature – there was by now already a 1.7IE ('Iniezione Elettronica') version on the market in Europe (though not in Great Britain). The odd feature is that the new 4 × 4 should be powered by an engine as small as the 1.3. But clearly, Alfa Romeo saw the justification for the smaller engine, almost certainly on the grounds that the cost of vehicle licensing in some European countries is based on engine size.

With the arrival of the new Sportwagons came minor modifications to the suspension to improve roadholding and compensate for the power steering now available on some models and standard on others. Again, considering the vehicle taxation system and catering for the Alfa owner who wanted a slightly smaller engine than the 1.7, a new version of the 33 1.5 was announced. This was the 33 1.5IE Saloon, which saw the introduction of the Bosch L3.1 Jetronic fuel injection system applied to the 1,490cc engine. In all other respects, the new car was identical to the 1.7IE, with the same standard of interior fit, the same body trim and finish, but with a slightly lower price tag.

All in all, the Alfa 33 has done the same as all of its predecessors since it was first

Filippo Surace, creator of the Arna and the highly successful Alfa 33 series of cars.

released in 1983. It has grown up, and now it stands much closer in body styling, standard of interior trim and performance envelope to the next car up the line, the highly successful Alfa 75 (which itself was a development of the Alfetta Saloon). The Alfa 33 1.7IE has a top speed of 118mph (189.8kph), matching the Alfa 75 1.8, whilst the 33 Boxer 16V's 129mph (207.4kph) comes very close to the 2.5i V6 and actually beats the 126mph (202.7kph) of the Alfa 75 2.0i Twin Spark. So the Alfa 33 seems set to continue in some form for a while yet, preserving the link with Rudolf Hruska's original concept which was brought to life in the Alfasud almost twenty years ago . . .

11 Alfas at Play – Racing and Rallying

Alfa Romeos have been competing on the roads and tracks of Europe almost from the very beginning of their existence, but throughout its history, Alfa Romeo *always* took its competitive activities seriously and used them as a means of demonstrating quality, reliability and durability. For example, in 1911, just a year after Anonima Lombarda Fabbrica Automobili was formed, Alfa 20/30s, driven by Franchini and Ronzoni, took part in the now-historic Targa Florio. Third and fourth places in the 1914 Coppa Florio confirmed Alfa's commitment to improving the breed through the medium of competition.

Down the years, Alfa Romeo has achieved unequalled success in long distance endurance racing. Before Word War II, only Bentley equalled the four-times victories at the Le Mans 24-hour Race. After winning the first World Grand Prix Championship, Alfa Romeo went to achieve an unmatched list of successes, which resulted in the formation of a very famous racing team, the Scuderia Ferrari. This team was created by another now-famous name: Enzo Ferrari, who had joined Alfa-Romeo as a test driver/mechanic, from which ranks Alfa-Romeo's racing drivers were drawn. Soon after joining the company, Ferrari became the team manager for Alfa-Romeo and began to build a team which became invincible in the world of motor racing.

It is impossible, within the context of a book of this kind and size, to give a complete account of Alfa Romeo competition successes. It is equally impossible to convey a true picture of the sheer hardship of running in many of the early pre-war races, leave alone winning them. These achievements demanded a level of reliability and durability in the cars, and sheer grit on the part of the drivers, that is almost unbelievable today. But Alfa Romeo had that kind of reliability and Enzo Ferrari that kind of grit. He had a totally free hand to run the team as Alfa Corse up to 1929, then was given the racing team on a plate to run under the banner of Scuderia Ferrari.

THE ROAD TO GRAND PRIX SUPREMACY

In the early post-Great War years, Enzo Ferrari recruited Vittorio Jano to Alfa-Romeo, who soon established himself as a talented designer. His first great success came after the P1 Grand Prix car, which was designed for the new 2-litre Grand Prix engine capacity limit and was to make its debut at the 1923 Gran Premio d'Italia at Monza. However, Ugo Sivocci lost his life testing one just before the race, so the whole Alfa-Romeo team was withdrawn in respect for their fallen hero. Motor racing had sportsmanship then. After the disastrous loss of Sivocci, the P1 was abandoned and Vittorio Jano had the job of designing a reliable Grand Prix car which would win races against all opposition.

This new two-seat Grand Prix car was the immortal Alfa-Romeo Type P2, which had its first outing in the 1924 Circuit of Cremona,

*After a convincing win in the 1924 Italian Grand Prix, Antonio Ascari is
helped from his P2; Vittorio Jano is on the left.*

where Antonio Ascari scored its first major victory. This was the car which won the first-ever Grand Prix World Championship and placed the name of Alfa-Romeo firmly on the list of great motor racing names, a legend in its own time. After the championship, Alfa-Romeo kept one P2 so, that when a suitable car was being sought for racing as late as 1930, two were bought back from private owners and re-bodied to make a new team of cars. So successful was the P2 still that Varzi and Tabacchi drove one to a magnificent outright victory in the 1930 Targa Florio. In that same year, Borzacchini won Alfa-Romeo's fifth Coppa Acerbo in a P2. This was true Championship stuff.

During 1927, the first of Jano's magnificent production six-cylinder engined cars took to the road. This was the 6c 1500 which,

in Sports and Super Sports form, had twin overhead camshafts. Enzo Ferrari drove one in 1927's Circuit of Modena, whilst Giuseppe Campari came second in the gruelling 1928 Targa Florio in another. In 1928, Alfa-Romeo scored its first victory in the world's toughest and greatest motor race, the Mille Miglia, with a 6c1500SS driven by Campari and Ramponi, who were followed into fourth place by Guidotti and Marinoni in a similar car. A few weeks after his Mille Miglia victory, Campari secured second place in the equally gruelling Targa Fiorio. In 1929, Giuseppe Campari and Giulio Ramponi won the Mille Miglia again, this time driving the natural successor to the 1500, the immortal Alfa-Romeo 1750. They were followed into second place by Varzi and Colombo in another 1750.

*Achille Varzi and co-driver Tabacchi
en route to victory in the 1930 Mille Miglia,
aboard a re-bodied P2.*

ALFA THE GREAT

The next decade, 1930 to 1940, was when Alfa-Romeo established a reputation as the maker of the world's greatest racing cars. Even when Adolf Hitler sponsored the rise of Mercédès-Benz and Auto-Union, Alfa-Romeo was still recognized as the artist of high speed motor cars and all across the Europe and North Africa, Alfa-Romeos were cheered on to victory after victory.

Among the catalogue of great racing drivers in the Alfa-Romeo fold during those years were such names as: Giuseppe Campari, Giulio Ramponi, Enzo Ferrari, Tazio Nuvolari, Achille Varzi, Count Gaston Brilli-Perri, the Honourable Brian Lewis, Tim Rose-Richards, Louis Chiron, Rudolf

Caracciola, Richard Seaman, Giuseppe Farina, Count Trossi, Clemente Biondetti, Carlo Pintacuda, Piero Taruffi and many others. This roll of honour was to confirm the legend that comes to mind even now, in the twilight of the twentieth century, whenever the name 'Alfa Romeo' is mentioned.

As the thirties dawned, Alfa-Romeo had already won more international motor races than any other Italian motor manufacturer and than most other European makers, too. By the end of that decade, Alfa-Romeo, in addition to all their Grand Prix victories, had established absolute mastery of the most important road races in Europe, winning no less than five Coppa Acerbos, four Le Mans, three Mille Miglias, two Targa Florios and an RAC Tourist Trophy Race. In the next decade, they won *seven* more Mille Miglias (every one between 1932 and 1938), *five* more Targa Florios and *four* more Coppa Acerbos. And then, the Honourable Brian Lewis won the International Trophy Race at Brooklands, Hans Ruesch and Richard Seaman ran away with the 1936 Donington Grand Prix, whilst Tazio Nuvolari won the 1936 Vanderbilt Cup in America, with Brivio coming home into third place.

THE BRIGHT NEW STAR

A most important pre-war race for Alfa-Romeo was the 1939 Coppa Acerbo, which later became the Pescara Grand Prix. Here, the 'Alfetta' single-seater scored its first resounding victory. In that race, Clemente Biondetti drove to a magnificent copy-book victory, followed by Carlo Pintacuda and Giuseppe Farina into second and third places. Developed largely by Gioacchino Colombo, these cars were so successful that they were to form the basis of Alfa Romeo's post-war attack on the Grand Prix world.

Gioacchino Colombo was a bright young engineer who had worked on the Alfetta design to race in the 1.5-litre 'Voiturette'

Sir Henry Birkin and Earl Howe broke Bentley's hold on Le Mans with a resounding win in 1931 aboard an Alfa Romeo 8c2300.

class of single-seat racing. But war curtailed the challenge, so the racing cars were locked in the workshops under the banking of Monza Park's racing track. In 1943 the Germans decided to use Monza Park as a military vehicle storage depot, causing panic at Alfa Romeo's factory, for Colombo visualized his precious racing cars being taken away as war booty. He therefore moved the whole collection of cars, their spare parts and mobile workshop support vehicle to the unlikely location of a cheese factory in Melzo, where everything was walled up for the duration!

When peace finally came to Europe and factories were repaired, Gioacchino Colombo recovered his racing team and materials from Melzo in readiness for the revival of motor racing. The new Grand Prix Formula allowed, from 1947, cars with unsupercharged engines of 4.5-litres capacity, or supercharged engines of 1.5-litres capacity. Alfa Romeo had a ready-made team to re-enter the fray, though some work was required before serious racing began.

Alfa Romeo's Board of Directors gave the go-ahead for the return to motor racing on the basis that no *new* design and build work was to be done. They approved Colombo's request for funding and materials to go to work on the 158 single-seaters, so he was now able to create a new Alfa Corse bent on victory. The new Grand Prix team featured four cars initially, from which, over the next six years, Alfa Corse swept the board.

Giuseppe Farina, Jean-Pierre Wimille and Count Trossi came first, second and third in Geneva's 1946 Grand Prix des Nations, then, by 1947, Alfa Romeo had squeezed 275bhp from the Alfetta engine and Trossi won the Italian Grand Prix, while Varzi won the Bari Grand Prix and Wimille the European. In 1948, they won the French, Italian, European and Monza Grands Prix, whilst Jean-Pierre Wimille and Chico Landi took a pair of pre-war Alfa 308 Grand Prix cars to first

---

Gioacchino Colombo

Some 20 miles to the north-west of Milan, in a small town called Legnano, Gioacchino Colombo was born in January 1903. Apprenticed to the Officine Franco Tosi, a local engineering company, he became a draughtsman and worked on diesel engine projects, as well as steam turbines.

In 1924, Colombo applied to take an entrance examination to join Società Anonima Ingegnere Nicola Romeo & C, seeing a prospect of advancing his career more quickly than in his home town. He felt that his work on steam turbines would help his career, since this was advanced engineering for its time. Early that year, his application was accepted and he was recruited into Vittorio Jano's design team to work on the P2 Grand Prix car.

Gioacchino Colombo rapidly established for himself a reputation of precision and speed in his drawings and in the work behind them. His theories were sound, and by 1928, he found himself appointed by Jano as chief draughtsman, with an ever-closer involvement in racing car design. Jano's involvement in the wider technical direction of truck and aero engine design and manufacture meant that he spent less time concerned with racing cars, leaving more and more to Colombo, who Jano once described as his right arm. Praise indeed!

As the racing activity was transferred to Scuderia Ferrari, so Jano reduced his personal involvement, leaving racing cars liaison between the factory and Modena to Colombo. It was during this time that this small, round, bald-headed man demonstrated his true abilities by designing the 308, the 312 and the 316 Grands Prix cars, as well as the vast bulk of the design, and certainly *all* the application drawings for the world-beating Alfetta Tipo 158, which became the first-ever Driver's World Championship mount.

Leaving Alfa Romeo for Ferrari, where he designed the V-12 engine refined by, and often erroneously credited to, Aurelio Lampredi, Gioacchino Colombo returned to Alfa Romeo to see his creation complete its quest for World Championship laurels. He left Alfa Romeo again to join Maserati; worked with Bugatti on the 251 project and then joined the motorcycle company MV, where he ended his career. Gioacchino Colombo died in 1987, his loss mourned by the many followers who thought him a genius.

---

and second places in Brazil's Sao Paolo Grand Prix. But after thirteen Grand Prix victories in a row, Alfa Romeo decided it was time for a rest, so they did not field a works team in 1949.

GRAND PRIX CHAMPIONS AGAIN – AND AGAIN

In 1949, the General Assembly of the FIA inaugurated a World Grand Prix Drivers' Championship for Formula 1 Grands Prix. This brought Alfa Romeo back to Grand Prix racing, with the old faithful Alfetta 158. By now, the 158/47 produced a quite amazing 350bhp at 8,600rpm. The Grand Prix d'Europe at Silverstone was first in the series, with Britain's Royal Family, headed by King George VI, in attendance. Fangio retired with a broken connecting rod, but Farina went through to win, with Fagioli in second place and British driver, Reg Parnell, in one of the older 275bhp cars, came home in third place to make it another Alfa Romeo 1-2-3.

Through the rest of that year, Alfa Romeos won the French Grand Prix, the Coppa Acerbo, the Bari Grand Prix, the Belgian, the Monaco, the Swiss Grands Prix, the Grand Prix des Nations at Geneva and the International Trophy Race at Silverstone. Since its first outing in 1938, the Alfetta 158 had competed in 39 premier events, winning 33 and taking 41 second or third places. And this was not the end.

The year 1951 brought the last Formula 1 Grand Prix version of the Alfetta, the Tipo

Fangio again, this time in a thoroughly wet 1951 Swiss Grand Prix, driving a 159. Once more, the Master won the race.

159. Gioacchino Colombo had left Alfa Romeo some four years before this last Alfa Romeo Grand Prix season, lured away to work with his old master, Enzo Ferrari, to develop the 4.5-litre Ferrari 375 Grand Prix car. In that intervening period, the two principal contenders for the Championship had been designed by the same man. But for 1951, Colombo was back and this last Alfetta was, to many, his finest piece of work. The engine produced 425bhp: this was to be Alfa Romeo's, and Juan Manuel Fangio's, finest year. Together, they went on to restore Alfa Romeo's immortality and secure another World Driver's Championship.

RACING AND RALLYING IN THE FIFTIES

Alfa Romeo withdrew from Grand Prix racing at the end of 1951, but they didn't withdraw from all forms of motor sport. The famous pre-war races were now the subject of their attention, the aim being to restore former glory in such events as the Targa Florio, the Mille Miglia and Le Mans. The Bornigia brothers won the 1950 Targa Florio with a 6c2500 Competizione Coupe, with JM Fangio third in a similar car, so starting a new train of sports car successes against the growing opposition of Ferrari, Maserati,

Aston Martin and Jaguar who were also all bent on winning races.

In 1951, a striking new Alfa Romeo took many an observer's breath away at the Mille Miglia. It was the 4500MM, a car built on the chassis of a pre-war Tipo 412, but with a body, by Vignale, which made the Jaguar XK120 look dated. It was driven in the race by Felice Bonetto and his co-driver Casnaghi, and came sixth overall, and third in the over-2-litre category, behind the best that Ferrari could produce.

With the experience gained from that Mille Miglia, Alfa Romeo went on to the 1953 event, where it entered three Type 6c3000CM Coupes, driven by Fangio, Kling and Sanesi. With a two-minute lead over Farina's Ferrari at Ravenna, Sanesi retired as he came out of Pescara. Kling quickly went to the front but, just before reaching Rome, he retired with a rear axle oil leak. Farina retired before Florence, so it was now up to Fangio, who had the lead as he left that city. But then, his left front wheel detached from the track rod, and he was steering on one wheel. Undeterred, he drove on, to be overtaken by Marzotto's Ferrari in the Appenines, where steering was all-important. But even with this setback, with characteristic courage and determination, Fangio finished second.

Alfa Romeo was now cutting back on all forms of motor racing, as the 1900 was in full production and the development of the Giulietta series was well advanced. Both demanded a great deal of attention, so Alfa Romeo took part in less races. They fielded Fangio and Sanesi in 6c3000CMs at Le Mans in 1953, though both retired. Then Fangio won the 1953 Supercortemaggiore Grand Prix at Merano, but a year later, Consalvo Sanesi almost lost his life in the same event as he went off at Ascari Bend. The car went up in flames and Sanesi was badly injured and burned. Alfa Romeo withdrew from motor racing then, leaving it to the priva-teers and their much-tuned production cars.

Rallying then began to grow in popularity as the nearest alternative form of motor sport, so Alfa Romeos began to appear in rallies. Consalvo Sanesi piloted a 1900 Sprint Coupe in the 1950 Stella Alpina, whilst a 1900TI Saloon won the 2-litre class of the 1953 Tour de France and another was third overall in the Giro di Sicilia. But racing still wasn't totally dead, one truly exciting result being the Sgorbati/Zanelli Giulietta Sprint finishing eleventh overall in the last but one, 1956, Mille Miglia.

THE RETURN ROAD TO FAME

In the late 1950s, the Zagato brothers took a Giulietta Sprint and re-bodied it as the Giulietta SZ. Some 200 were built for homo-logation purposes, so that the racing and rallying fraternities could use them as production cars. An early SZ victory was that of Costen and de Langeneste in the 1958 Coupe Internationale des Alpes, whilst Sprint Zagatos took second and third places in the 1,300cc class of the 1960 Targa Florio. Another Alpine Rally success was the Rolland/Augois class win in 1963.

This led to the TZ, the Tubolare Zagato. The TZ was produced by a small engineering firm in Udine, known as Delta, the offshoot of an Alfa Romeo dealership run by two brothers named Chizzola. One of them teamed up with Ingegnere Carlo Chiti to form Delta and build a tubular-framed Zagato-bodied coupe with much-developed Giulia mechanicals. They were given the task of building 100 cars for homologation, since there was no room at Portello to build them and Alfa Romeo's move to Arese was in process.

The TZ was an immediate success and went on to win many races in both of its developed forms, as the TZ1 and TZ2. So successful was the TZ1 that, when Alfa Romeo decided in 1964 that it was time to renew works

Rolland and Augois took this Giulia SZ to an Alpine Cup in the 1963 Coupe Internationale des Alpes.

The TZ2 prototype in the 1965 Circuit of Mugello, bringing a class win for Teodore Zeccoli.

patronage of motor racing, they bought out the interests of Delta and re-organized it as Autodelta under the authority of Carlo Chiti. The TZ2 was a lowered and lighter weight development of the TZ with a fibreglass body. Called the 'mini-GTO' the TZs were every bit the equal of the Ferrari GTO in their capacity class and, along with the Giulia GTAs, won most of the events they entered and provided a step to fame for such names as Andrea de Adamich, Giancarlo Baghetti, Lorenzo Bandini, Lucien Bianchi, Spartaco Dini, Nanni Galli, Jochen Rindt, Jean Rolland and Nino Vaccarella.

REVIVING THE LEGEND – THE ALFA 33

As the TZs and GTAs were reviving the Alfa Romeo legend, another car was to appear in 1967 which, in the ensuing ten years, would have a profound effect on the motor racing world and the reputation of Alfa Romeo. That car first appeared in open two-seater

form and was to be called the Tipo 105.33, or 'Alfa 33', and was announced to the press in March 1967. A mid-engined car, the prototype was powered by a GTA engine, but the unit designed for the new car was a 2-litre V-8 which produced a tremendous 270bhp.

Through the remaining years of the 1960s, the T33 was to gain fame in sports and prototype racing for its capacity to take on the giants – who, at this time, were Ferrari and Porsche. In 1973, Alfa Romeo produced the car which would finally revive the legend for them as a sports car champion. This was the 33TT12, which practised in the 1973 Spa-Francorchamps 1,000 kilometres, but ran 'for real' in that year's Targa Florio. However, Clay Regazzoni spun his 33TT12 in a spectacular fashion and went down a mountain in it, climbing out and walking away unhurt from the wrecked car, whilst Andrea de Adamich had a massive shunt into a Lancia which pulled out in front of him.

The 1974 season was not eventful for Alfa

*Giancarlo Baghetti in the T33 'Periscopica' prototype at the 1967 Nürburgring
1,000 kilometres.*

Romeo, but careful development of the 33TT12 brought an Alfa 1-2-3 in the Monza 1,000 kilometre Race on Liberation Day, 25 April, whilst the Nürburgring 750 kilometres saw an Alfa second place and in the Imola '1,000', a pair of 33TT12s were second and third. In 1975, a German named Willi Kauhsen put up the funds to run the team. In the first race of that year, the Circuit of Mugello, two 33s finished second and fourth. At Dijon-Prenais, Arturo Merzario and Jacques Lafitte ran away with the 800-kilometre race, while Derek Bell and Henri Pescarolo managed fourth place in the same race, despite having to change a front wheel bearing on the way.

Alfa 33TT12s romped away with the 1975 Monza '1,000', the Coppa Florio, the Nürburgring '1,000' and the Austrian '600' races, as well as the Watkins Glen Six Hours, taking the World Championships of Makes to Arese with ease. Alfa Romeo was now ready to return to Formula 1 Grand Prix racing.

BACK TO GRAND PRIX AND ANOTHER SPORTS CAR CHAMPIONSHIP

Returning to Grand Prix racing after twenty-five years, Alfa Romeo took a very cautious line, preferring to provide the power train for the British-based Brabham team, with Brazilian Carlos Pace and Argentinian Carlos Reutemann driving the BT45s which were powered with specially developed flat-twelve Alfa Romeo engines. Victory in Grand Prix racing was elusive, their first win coming in Sweden at the 1978 Grand Prix, with the infamous 'fan' car. The latter was a very controversial machine with a fan behind the gearbox, designed to extract heat, and air, from under the car, so helping the down-forces to keep the car on the track, rather along the lines of the American Chapparal sports car of almost a decade before.

In the meantime, Alfa Romeo had returned to sports car racing in 1977, determined to repeat their 1975 success with the Alfa 33s. Eight races were to be fought, using a new monocoque construction car called the 33SC12, with three new drivers joining Arturo Merzario. These were: Vittorio Bramabilla, Jean-Pierre Jarier and John Watson. First race of the year was the Dijon '500', where the Jarier/Watson car put up the fastest lap, but failed to finish, though Merzario and Brambilla stormed to victory. Alfa Romeos were piloted to victory in the Monza '500', the Vallelunga '400', the Coppa Florio, the Premio Costa del Sol, the Paul Ricard 500 kilometres and the Imola '250', where the three 33SC12s were the fastest cars in the field.

The last event in the World Sports Car Constructors' Championship was the Salzburger Feistpielpreis at the Salzburgring and it was here that the turbocharged T33SC12 was first seen, driven by Arturo Merzario. The race was won by Vittorio Brambilla's 33SC12, Merzario was second and the Dini/Francia car third. Alfa Romeo had won its second Constructors' Championship.

THE END OF GRAND PRIX AND RACING TODAY

Alfa Romeo continued Grand Prix racing with dogged determination, but victory seemed to elude them all the way. They built their own cars and stuck with it through the turbocharged period, building some magnificent engines, but never securing the reliability or pace essential to victory. So, by 1985, with the last Benetton-Alfa, the company decided to quit, supplying engines to entrants but fielding no cars of their own. The last of those was Ligier, who contracted to use the 415T engine, but switched to BMW at the last minute. On the other hand, Formula 3 has been a huge success for Alfa Romeo, along with sports car and production saloon car racing.

In 1988, Alfa Romeo won the European

A GTV-6 2.5 in action at Donington Park.

Touring Car Championship with the Alfa 75. In 1989 they were ready to field a team of cars in the 'Silhouette' Series, but other makers backed away, so the series was abandoned. The new Alfa Romeo 3.5-litre V-10 engine was available for racing use, but went nowhere. However, a new Grand Prix style V-8 engine was developed for racing in the North American CART Series and has been fielded with mixed success.

Today, Alfa Romeos of all sorts and sizes feature regularly in club racing, much of it sponsored with the Alfa Romeo Owners' Club of Great Britain. It is certainly true to say that every Alfa Romeo engine currently in production has been raced at some time – even on water, as they are now featuring strongly in the R/2000N powerboat racing series. What an acclamation! What a range of engines! What a history! Derived from the production four-cylinder twin-cam unit, the Alfa Romeo Formula 3 engine powered no less than 80 victories in the decade between 1980 and 1990.

12 Alfa Romeo – Today and Tomorrow

There is no doubt that, even under Fiat ownership, the name 'Alfa Romeo' still conjures up in the mind an image of fast, sporty cars. And, to a large extent, Alfa-Lancia SpA works hard to maintain that image. In the face of all suspicions that Fiat's take-over would be the death-knell of Alfa Romeo, it continues to offer its own product, designed by its own team, and is left very much to itself in terms of what it does and how it does it. The signal difference now is the method. Fiat's influence has improved production techniques and reduced waste. The movement of some Lancia products into Arese simply improved the utilization of factory space and manpower, so paving the way for Alfa-Lancia to move back into profit.

How has this affected Alfa Romeo? Well, to begin with, it has had a marked effect on quality control within the manufacturing facility. It has enabled designers to establish design features with less limitations upon them. And it has resulted in still better cars leaving the Alfa Romeo factories. Fiat itself has taken over the control of distribution in Britain and North America and has analysed the specific target markets at which Alfa Romeos should be aimed, so as to improve sales.

Fiat has seen distinct market sectors at which the products of its group companies should be targeted, recognizing brand loyalties and maximizing its opportunities around them. Alfa Romeo in particular has benefited from this course of action, for its product quality has settled down to a high level and its products are priced to place them in their target markets. In Great Britain, that means the Alfa 33 spearheads the smaller sector of the Alfa range, with the 33 Boxer 16V Permanent Four as its flagship. This is backed up by the Spider, for which Alfa Romeo recognizes Britain as a special market place, open sports cars having always been particularly popular in the British market. The Alfetta has gone, sadly, as has the Sprint, and neither the ES30 Zagato Coupe nor the Proteo offer a very suitable replacement, being limited in volume and expensive.

THE CURRENT PRODUCT RANGE

Alfa Romeo's current product range encompasses many cars not included within the scope of this book. Like most international car makers of repute, the Alfa range has a top-of-the-line executive saloon in the Alfa 164 3.0V6 Lusso, a four-door Pininfarina design which shares a basic body shell with the Fiat Croma, the Lancia Thema and Sweden's Saab 9000CD. The body panels of each car are sufficiently different from each other to allow the untrained eye to perceive them as four distinctly different cars – which, mechanically, they are. It's just another aspect of Fiat's broader conceptual thinking.

The 164 is a front-wheel-drive transverse-engined car, with the smallest of the range having the long-established 1.8-litre Alfa Romeo four-cylinder engine, which in this

The Alfa Romeo four-cam 16-valve Boxer engine.

case is turbocharged. Then there's a 2-litre Twin Spark, a 2.5-litre diesel and the 3.0V6. Hard on the 164's heels comes the Alfa 75, a car specifically designed to mark the 75th Anniversary of Alfa Romeo and introduced in 1985. It was this car which heralded the turn-round of Alfa Romeo's fortunes – the car upon which much attention was focussed after the Fiat take-over, and the car which Alfa Romeo has fielded in the European Touring Car Championships, acquitting itself outstandingly well in both the Italian Touring Car Series and the European Series.

A naturally aspirated 1.8 sits at the bottom of the range of Alfa 75s, with a 2.0 Twin Spark next. The 2.0 Twin Spark Veloce is an upbeat version of the Twin Spark, with alloy road wheels, front air dam and body side-skirts. Next up the line is the first car Alfa Romeo ever offered with automatic transmissions as standard equipment, the 2.5V6 Automatic, which also now comes in Veloce form, as does the top-of-the-range 75 model, the 3.0V6. All these cars carry a six-year anti-corrosion warranty. The key body panels are zincrometal coated and electro-galvanized, whilst the computer-aided design programme at Arese ensures the absolute minimum of built-in water traps to reduce corrosion risks. After cleaning and degreasing, the box sections in the body structure are wax-injected, whilst the whole underside of every car is treated to a thick urethane coating to reduce stone chip damage. These are cars as rust-proof and durable as Alfa Romeo can make them.

The 1990 Alfa 33s, the 1.7IE at the rear and the Boxer 16V in front.

SO WHAT'S NEXT?

Sadly, the Sprint and the Alfetta GTV have gone, leaving Alfa Romeo with only the Spider to defend its honour in the sports car arena for the time being. So one particular sector of the market, the three-door four-seat hatchback, is no longer served by Arese. And it may not be for some time to come, though

The elegant new Alfa Romeo Spider 2.0.

the 16-valve boxer engine is surely not destined only to power a saloon car, albeit a pretty hairy one – is it? But wait, for it's not quite true that there is *no* sporting coupe at all in the Alfa range! If you were quick enough to have placed your name on the list, and you could afford the price, you might have been lucky to get an order in for the limited edition ES30 Sprint Zagato Coupe, which in Britain hit the market in 1990 on a price tag of £40,000. And what a limited edition!

Mechanically, the SZ has its origins in the Alfetta, with a longitudinally disposed front-mounted engine driving the rear wheels by means of the tried and tested transaxle. Destined to be only built in left-hand-drive form, the engine chosen for this most exciting of Alfa Romeos was the 3-litre V-6, 'tweaked' to produce over 200bhp. Strictly a two-seater, the SZ has only enough room for its occupants, a couple of modest parcels or overnight bags behind the seats and a 'get-you-home' spare wheel.

Designed by Alfa Romeo's own team, led by Walter de Silva, and developed with Carrozzeria Zagato, the ES30 was the result of several paper images converted ultimately into just two full-size models. One had the bold, aggressive line committed to the production prototype, and known as the 'B' Type, whilst the other had a softer line and was called the 'A' Type. The decision was made in favour of the design chosen, the 'B' Type, for its boldness of style, which was guaranteed to make it stand out in the crowd.

Given that the styling of this car has been wind-tunnel tested to produce a drag coefficient of less than 0.30, it is a fact that its lines will not appeal to every individual who might aspire to owning a 150mph Alfa Romeo sports coupe. It is also true to say that

Another exciting Alfa is the ES30 Zagato Coupe, known as the SZ and built in limited numbers through 1989 and 1990.

This view of the SZ shows off its thoroughly aggressive lines.

the Type 'A' design was much easier on the eye and might even have been easier to manufacture the mould tools for, since all the body panels are made from Modar (a carbon fibre reinforced plastic material conceived by ICI and moulded by a company called Carplast of Piacenza, then glued to the steel cage-type chassis).

BUILDING AND DRIVING THE ES30 SPRINT ZAGATO

The development programme for the ES30 took nineteen months from a clean sheet of paper to the first complete approved prototype, revealed in 1988, then a further five months to start production of the definitive vehicle, which was scheduled to be completed in Spring 1989. The Geneva Motor Show of March 1989 fulfilled the promise, with the sixth car built, that definitive prototype, on display there. It took the motoring world by storm.

Production of the steel cage-type chassis was entrusted to Carrozzeria Zagato. After manufacture, it was decreed that the shell should go to Arese for anti-corrosion treatment, including galvanizing and electrophoretic coating. The mechanical components and running gear were then built up and installed, after which the Modar and glassfibre panels were bonded with a high-pressure adhesive to the steel base and the whole was painted by Zagato in their very modern facility at Terrazo di Rho, near Milan. The body employs three composite materials: a cold injection moulded composite containing Modar (a thermosetting metacrylic resin) and glassfibre, Kevlar (a carbon-reinforced aramidic resin plastic) and simple glassfibre, whilst the roof panel is aluminium. The interior of the SZ is the work of the Zagato team and the production plan was for three to four cars per day, taking just over a year for the total run.

Specification – Alfa Romeo Tipo ES30 Sprint Zagato Coupe

Model ES30 Sprint Zagato 'SZ'
Year 1989–on

Type 2-seat coupe
Wheelbase 2,510mm
Track 1,396mm (F); 1,382mm (R)
Tyre sizes 205/55ZR × 16 (F); 225/50ZR × 16 (R)
Brakes 284mm (F) and 250mm (R) vented discs
Suspension Co-axial spring/damper strut units in front with parallel transverse links and anti-roll bar, de Dion rear with coverging rods and Watts linkage and co-axial helical coil spring/damper units
Engine 2,959cc single ohc per bank
No. of cylinders 6 in vee formation at 60 degrees
Bore/stroke 93mm × 72.6mm
Induction Fuel injection
Ignition Electronic
Power output 210bhp @ 6,200rpm
Transmission 5-speed gearbox in unit with rear axle, driving rear wheels
Gear ratios 1st 11.238:1; 2nd 6.723:1; 3rd 4.792:1; 5th 3.049:1; reverse 11.73:1
Maximum Road Speed 153mph (245kph)
Mph per 1,000rpm 23.81mph (38.1kph) in top gear

Versions catalogued Sprint Zagato Coupe

With a wheelbase of 8ft (2,510mm) and a track of a little more than 4.5ft (1,400mm), the SZ on the road is a true sports car. Its styling is thoroughly functional, if a little abrupt, and with an almost 'ground-effect' body, its road adhesion (thus cornering and handling) is superb. The specially designed Pirelli 'P Zero' tyres are on 16in rims, with rears of 225/50 size and 205/50 fronts, justifying the use of servo-assisted rack-and-pinion power steering. Front suspension uses independent struts with transverse links and damping by double-acting shock absorbers. Straight from the Alfetta comes the de Dion rear end, with converging rods and Watts linkage, the coil springs being mounted co-axially with the shock absorbers. An adjustable ride height, with a stroke of 40mm, completes the suspension.

Road test reports credit the SZ with outstanding, road-hugging, handling and describe the car as 'totally predictable' in the dry, with just enough 'feel' to ensure that you know exactly where the power-steered front tyres are at any time. In the wet, it seems, the car is a little more of a handful, though this may have something to do with the tyres more than chassis design configuration. With a 0–60mph (0–100kph) time of seven seconds and a top speed of over 145mph (235kph), this is a truly outstanding limited edition, especially since the price tag, within the scheme of things, is really quite modest. Any production car with a power-to-weight ratio of almost 150bhp per ton has to be a pretty exciting prospect for the price of this one.

Whilst one could write a complete book on this quite unique and thoroughly exciting car, surely the true heir of the Alfetta and the Alfa Romeo enigma, we must move on. Indeed, someone *has* produced a volume dedicated to the ES30, entitled simply 'Alfa Romeo SZ', but we now must look at the other prospects awaited from the drawing boards of Arese.

TOMORROW'S ALFA ROMEOS?

Like any internationally renowned motor manufacturer, Alfa Romeo is not likely to release to the world at large what its specific plans are too early in the gameplan. That's not least because it does not want good ideas to be 'poached' by less than scrupulous competitors, nor does it want to set too many ideas in firm process before it has to, in case of new developments or legislation. How-

ever, in a series of press interviews in 1990, Alfa Romeo's Managing Director, Giovanbattista Razelli, lifted the lid from a few glimpses of what might be in the future of one of Italy's, indeed the world's, most respected car makers.

For example, Razelli, who took control of Alfa Romeo in 1989, was resolved from the beginning to continue the path of quality improvement embarked upon by his predecessors and has publicly stated his intention to raise the profile of Alfa Romeo in the market place. With a background of running the turbulent Ferrari operation, he has to have a better-than-even chance of success. With Arese and Pomigliano d'Arco running at capacity, thanks partly to the absorption of Lancia production in both plants, and an 8.7 per cent volume increase on Alfa Romeo's own model range in 1989, with further improvements in 1990, it looks as though Signor Razelli has already made his mark.

The year 1990 saw the introduction of the revamped Alfa Romeo Spider in both 1.6-litre and 2-litre versions, as well as the 16-valve Alfa 33 and a new version of the top-of-the-range model, the 164 Quadrifoglio Verde (Green Cloverleaf). Amidst all this, the ES30 Sprint Zagato Coupe has also reached production. Giovanbattista Razelli has made it very plain that he expects Alfa Romeo cars not just to equal their competitors in performance potential (which is not a problem for Arese), but that he expects, and believes, that Alfa Romeo product quality does and will equal any competitor.

It is also clear that the Alfa 75's successor will be here by the time you read this with, if the images released from Arese so far are anything to go on, a softer line and more rounded, but not quite 'jelly mould' form. 'Time is needed to create new legends', says Razelli, 'and it is creating new legends that is the task ahead'. That encapsulates the whole attitude of revival currently running

Announced at the 1991 Geneva Motor Show, this is the 164-based Proteo four-wheel-drive prototype.

A plan view of the Proteo, showing its 'coke-bottle' waisting and four-wheel-drive layout with the transverse V-6 engine.

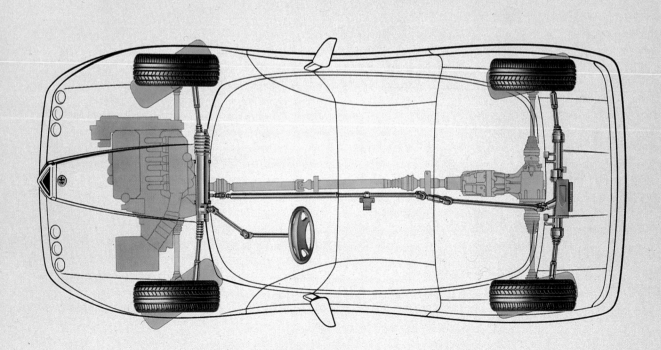

*The single overhead-cam-per-bank V-6 engine used in the 164 Saloon and the
SZ Coupe. The Proteo used a four-cam version (two-per-bank).*

The Alfa 33 Sportwagon 1.7.

through Alfa Romeo at all levels and, as long as it continues, then you will see exciting new cars leaving the gates of Arese and Pomigliano d'Arco.

There have also been many rumours of what might succeed the SZ, since every Alfa Romeo enthusiast expects a coupe somewhere in the range. So far, Signor Razelli has only leaked that a future volume-produced coupe is more likely to be front-engined rather than mid-engined and could share minor components with a future Maserati. But it will not be two old adversaries brought together in a badge-engineered exercise. It was thought that the 3.5-litre V-10 engine, produced originally for Formula 1, then the abortive Pro-Car Series 164, could be revived for use in this new coupe. But the 1991 Geneva Motor Show revealed another development prototype, upmarket of the SZ, powered by a version of the much-respected V-6 engine, but now in quad-cam form, with two camshafts per cylinder bank.

Four-wheel drives and station wagons seem hardly to fit the image of a car maker with the reputation of Alfa Romeo, a company which has a glorious history of battle in the Grands Prix and epic road races of the world, but four-wheel drive is now fashionable in the world of high performance cars. So this magnificent new coupe, the Alfa Romeo 'Proteo', has four-wheel drive, and four-wheeled steering too. Three prototypes were built initially and one was displayed at Geneva, drawing great interest from press and public alike. Built on a shortened 164 floorpan, and with a 260bhp engine, the 'Proteo' is a sports car in the true Alfa Romeo tradition.

Styled very much in the idiom of the SZ, though of softer line and easier on the eye, this new 164 Super Coupe is the test-bed for things to come. For the moment, though, the 33 remains the only 4 × 4 in Alfa Romeo's portfolio. In the same Geneva Show as revealed the 164 Coupe, the 33S Permanent 4 was also announced, elevating the 33 4 × 4 to a higher market plane.

The 75 has been offered as a Sportwagon, along with the 33, the latter being offered still as a 4 × 4 too. But there are few signs of any expansion into Sportwagons elsewhere within the product range. However, the 75's successor is already destined to be offered in two- and four-wheel drive form, when it comes. Styling exercises for the new model display a much more rounded design than its almost razor-edged forebear, with a few characteristics which will identify it with the SZ generation of Alfa Romeo styling, though built on the Fiat 'Tipo' floorpan.

The production target set for Alfa Romeo in 1990, when the company emerged from the dark tunnel of loss-making into profit, was 350,000 cars a year within the current decade, and within that plan, there are clearly more exciting new products on the horizon. It seems we will almost certainly see the Alfa 75's successor during 1992 and we *may* see a new Spider in 1993. A two-door version of the 33 was promised by Signor Razelli, though the Alfa 33 saloon will clearly soldier on for a few years yet, having only recently been revamped and endowed with the 16-valve four-cam engine.

ENGINES AND ALFA CORSE

Ever since Vittorio Jano's magic and triumphant P2, engines have always been the strong suit in Alfa Romeo's development programme. The one engine which has been the subject of most development is the one which runs through the whole of this story, the in-line four-cylinder unit which evolved from the 1,290cc Giulietta engine of the 1950s. It has today become the 2.0 Twin Spark, which 'grew up' through the 1600, the 1750 and the original series 2000, to its present stage, where it powers the Alfa 75 and the Alfa 164. That same engine must surely find its way into the next Spider, too.

Three different cylinder heads have been produced in recent times for the 2.0 engine; a two-plug refinement of the two-valve-per-cylinder single plug head in use on the Spider engine, and a three-valve-per-cylinder twin-plug with two inlet valves and a single exhaust valve. The third has two inlet and two exhaust valves, but only one spark plug, simply because there isn't enough room in the combustion chamber for two. Another feature is the 'Lamellare' multiple reed valve, designed to be placed in the inlet port of the cylinder head to improve the atomization of the fuel/air mixture into the combustion chamber. The resulting more complete detonation of the gases produces a better power output for a specific fuel consumption, as well as giving a cleaner and leaner burning engine.

Alfa Romeo's V-6 power unit first appeared in the Alfa Six Saloon, then the Alfa 90 and the Alfetta GTV-6 as a 2.5-litre 160bhp unit. With the arrival in 1985 of the Alfa 75, it was enlarged to 2,959cc and installed in the top model of that range. In developed form, and rotated through 90 degrees, it went into the magnificent 164 Saloon, then twisted back to a longitudinal position to go into 'Il Monstro' as the SZ Coupe became known. In the Alfa 164 Quadrifoglio, this engine produces 200bhp, whereas 210bhp is extracted from it in its SZ form and 260bhp in quad-cam form for the Proteo.

'All Alfa Romeo engines are raced', quoted Ingegnere Razelli in a 1990 press interview. That is a tremendous commitment to the development of the most effective and efficient power units. Racing has improved the pedigree of *all* Alfa Romeo production engines, including the Boxer Four single and twin-cam per bank types, the in-line four from the original 1300 to the present-day 2-litre Twin Spark unit in Touring Car and International Formula 3, as well as having risen to supremacy in the Italian R2000/N speedboat series. Then the V-6 has seen competition in 2.5-litre and 3-litre forms through the Alfetta GTV-6 and the ETC Alfa 75s.

A most exciting development during 1989 was the V-8 CART engine, developed specially for racing in the USA's Champion Auto Racing Team Series. This is the US' answer to the European Formula 1 Grand Prix, except that the engines are limited to 2.65 litres capacity, may have a maximum eight cylinders and are allowed to be turbocharged. In 1990, the CART-racing Alfa Romeo engine of 2,648cc was combined with a March chassis to create the March-Alfa CA90. With Weber Marelli fuel injection and a Garrett turbocharger, this fine racing engine ran to 11,500rpm and gave over 700bhp. Sadly, the chassis seemed unable to match the performance of the engine, leaving Alfa Romeo among the also-rans instead of winning races, where it deserved to be. A five-valve-per-cylinder head for the engine was well advanced as this book went to press, so clearly Alfa Romeo doesn't intend to leave it there.

Most exciting of all though is the story that Alfa Romeo will be contesting the World Sports Car Endurance. Championship in Group C racing when the new formula becomes effective in 1992, with a capacity limit of 3,500cc. This exciting series could see contests between Alfa Romeo, Jaguar, Mercédès-Benz and Peugeot among the European car makers, with Nissan and Toyota from the Orient. Shall we see a revival of Alfa Romeo's sports car racing fortunes to match the great era of the 33TT12s and 33SC12s? Let us hope so.

Quoting Ingegnere Giovanbattista Razelli: 'Racing is of strategic and fundamental importance for Alfa Romeo, so Alfa Corse will be our right arm again.' With that kind of fighting talk, it is clear that Alfa Romeo is destined to remain a force to be reckoned with in all the forms of motor racing in which it engages today. The raised profile to which Razelli has referred in the past will surely come as a consequence of competitive success – again. Indeed, the revival of a true legend.

13 Rust, Restoration and Ownership

'CAVEAT EMPTOR'

Owning an Alfa Romeo is great fun, but it can also be a little precarious, especially if you don't know what you're looking for when you go out to buy your first-ever Alfa. Virtually *all* post-war Alfa Romeos, almost regardless of age, are prone to serious damage from corrosion, though the newer cars are certainly much better than ever their predecessors were. All new Alfas carry a six-year rust penetration guarantee, which undertakes rectification work at the cost of the manufacturer if rust has actually broken through the surface within a six-year period. Of course, that guarantee has caveats, the main one being that the car has to be regularly inspected by an authorized Alfa Romeo dealer and checked against a specific inspection programme.

Quite rightly, the six-year anti-corrosion guarantee is considered a superb advance in consumer protection. 'That's fine,' you'll say, 'if I want to buy a new 164, an Alfa 75 or a new 33. But what about that pretty smart-looking 1959 Giulietta Spyder, or a 1980 Alfasud, or a Bertone-bodied 2600 Sprint?'. Well, the only thing you have to fall back on as you seek to buy one of these wonders from Italy's past is a phrase from Italy's past: 'Caveat emptor', or 'Buyer beware'!

FINDING THE RUST-BUG

Whatever model of post-war Alfa Romeo you choose to buy, you can reckon that, if it is more than three or four years old, you'll have to do work on it to bring it up to acceptable condition. When you examine a car with a view to buying it, check the bodywork very thoroughly. First thing to do is to check the drain holes to make sure they've not been allowed to clog up. Front wings (or fenders, dependent upon which part of the world you sit in as you read this) generally suffer quite badly behind the wheel arches. Doors are almost always corroded at their bottom edges, whilst boot (or 'trunk') lids and tailgates also deteriorate as the consequence of years lying in pools of water at their bottom edges.

When you've had your superficial look at the panels, many of which will be detachable and replaceable, you need to examine the base structure to see if the car is worth all the expenditure you are about to lavish on it. So get the car up on a lift, where you can examine it in safety, with the benefit of a decent inspection lamp. Go down the floor panels with a fine screwdriver, prodding in odd places (usually around the folds which place reinforcing ribs in the structure itself) and gently try to jab holes in it. If your screwdriver goes through easily in several places, abandon it and invite the car's owner to take it away before it falls to pieces on you.

Cars with McPherson strut front suspension units need to be very carefully checked around the edges of the top mounting plate, where it is joined to the inner wing panel, for there is often a layer of sealing compound covering the beginnings of a split between two pieces of metal. That can often result in

This grubby Alfasud is the 1983 example which Your Classic *magazine,*
whose photos these are, took to Alfa Romeo (Great Britain) Ltd's workshops at
Dover for total restoration by AR (GB). The next shot shows the badly
deteriorated panels being removed and then the car ready for re-build. After
that, new panels are added to bring the car back to shape, then the bodyshell
is repainted and prepared for all the mechanical bits to be put back on.

an actual parting of metal, causing all kinds of problems, if not an accident, in its wake. So check your prospective car with meticulous caution. Make sure, as far as you can, that the damage through deterioration is limited to the non-structural metalwork, generally the visible panels on the outside of the car, for if it is structural, it can cost a lot of money to put right – more, perhaps, than the car is worth.

CHOOSING YOUR ALFA ROMEO

Before you can choose what Alfa Romeo you might want to buy (of the three basic types covered by this book that is), you need to decide whether it is an open car or a closed car that best suits your needs. If it is an open car, then you still have a fairly wide choice of models within the Spider line, provided you don't want more than two seats. If you *do* need more than two seats, then your choice between open and closed car is eliminated. However, you *still* have a choice of three basic cars, in the Alfasud Saloon, the Alfetta GT up to GTV-6 and the Alfasud Sprint or Alfa Romeo Sprint, dependent upon your year of choice in the latter case.

All the closed cars have at least four seats and all have reasonable rear-seat headroom, though the coupes are obviously slightly less well-endowed with space for the taller rear-seat passenger than the Alfasud Saloon. As for doors, would you believe that you can choose, from three closed Alfa Romeo models, two, three, four or five doors. So there you are: spoilt for choice. What's more, whichever one you choose from this limited selection, you will almost certainly never regret it from the driving seat.

Your own particular driving technique will almost certainly influence your choice. If you like tail-hanging rear-wheel drives, then don't even choose an Alfa Romeo, because most Alfas have positive roadholding with

little perceptible over- or understeer as long as you're in control. Not many people looking for an Alfa Romeo will have no idea whether they prefer front- or rear-wheel drive, but if you really *don't* know and you want to make your first incursion into the world of the *Alfisti*, then ignore the pundits and go for a relatively inexpensive Alfasud or Sprint.

If you want just four seats and don't want to spend large wedges of cash, you could do much worse than a Sprint, which was in production up to 1989. By that time, too, it was a pretty solid motor car and, with the exception of the rear spoiler, retained the attractive appearance possessed of the earlier Alfasud Sprint coupes. Five seats means the Alfasud Saloon or Hatchback and, of course, an older car, since the Alfasud went out of production in 1983.

Looking at the five-seat question, it is fair to say that the rear seating space in both the Sprint and its larger-engined sibling, the Alfetta GTV, is adequate for three adults over short distances and roomy enough for three children. But then, if you've got three kids, you might think about the more recent Alfa 33 Sportwagon, which is a 'grown up' Alfasud anyway, endowed with lots of space for kids in the back. So, presuming that you've sorted out the matters of how many seats, open or closed, small engine or large, let us now consider the pros and cons of each model and its variations.

ASSESSING THE SPIDER SERIES

As we've already established, the modern Alfa Romeo Spider began as a variant of the Giulietta as long ago as 1955. It is a creditable reflection upon the design skills and artistry of Pininfarina that this little car does not look particularly out of date even now, more than thirty-five years later. It is still more of a credit to Pininfarina that the car's direct successor continues in production and, since the 1990 introduction of the latest variant, seems set for a few more years' sales yet.

One of the most amazing features of the original Giulietta Spider was, and is, its performance for a 1,290cc power unit. Even compared with so-called sports cars of twenty years more recent production, the performance of this spirited little car remains outstanding. With a maximum speed of over 100mph (160kph) and roadholding to match, this little car remains, for the author at least, the most exciting and desirable of all the Spiders, with the possible single exception of the larger-engined Giulia version. A 'mini-Ferrari Spyder' is how it has been described and that is very much how the car impresses on the first drive. It is lively, manageable and great fun, though clearly it doesn't have the raw 'guts' of the Modena machine.

Since the introduction of the Spyder 1600 Duetto, little has changed under the skin of the Spider series, except engine sizes, power outputs and, perhaps, the odd spring rate and item of suspension geometry. It is an established fact that this approach has been one of the strong features of attraction in the Spider, endorsing the philosophy: 'Why change the recipe when the product is perfectly good?' So, the key question in determining which variant to buy is twofold: 'Which one do you most like the look of and how much money do you want to spend?' The irony is that you could now spend overall as much, or more, on a driveable but not concours standard Giulietta Spider as you would on a brand new Spider 2000.

Driving any Spider is fun, with superb handling and roadholding, though the earlier cars might draw a little benefit from the use of slightly wider rims to accommodate 80 per cent aspect ratio tyres. By this method, you increase the 'footprint' of tyre surface contact area on the road, without overstressing or doing damage to suspension parts and without seriously affecting the steering characteristics of your car.

Generally, Alfa Romeos are thought to have been better tyred than most, but a little extra grip can still help in those potentially tricky situations drivers find themselves in from time to time. The only things against the earlier Spiders are the scarcity of spare parts now, especially body parts, and the problems associated with Italian chrome plating. All in all, if you want a realistically priced, enjoyable open two-seat sports car, and you are prepared to take steps to protect against continuing rust, then you'll be very unlikely to be able to better the Alfa Romeo Spider.

EYEING UP THE ALFASUD AND SPRINT

If you have decided that you want to buy a front-wheel-drive Alfa Romeo, then your choice becomes pretty simple since, as far as this book is concerned, there is only the Alfasud Saloon or Alfasud/Alfa Romeo Sprint Coupe. In either case, the basic advice as to what to buy is the same – buy the latest car you can possibly afford, since the early rust problems were somewhat more serious than those with later models.

Regardless of which variant of Saloon or Sprint you choose, the basic areas of rust are much the same. Check very carefully the front windscreen pillars and front wings. The windscreen pillars faced two problems:

1. The screens were not always fitted with the necessary accuracy, so leaked water into the metal sub-structure, furthering rusting under the surface.
2. The trim clips on the bottom corners of the screen sometimes damaged the paintwork as they were fitted, leaving a bare patch just ready to rust away and weaken the whole front structure of the car.

Now, if you are looking for a two-door saloon or three-door hatchback (TI models fall into

*A well-kept and unrestored Alfetta GTV-6. (Inset) The GTV-6
from its most attractive angle. This is the author's own car.*

this category), check the doors very carefully. This advice also covers the Sprint models, since they, too, had long and heavy doors. The problem is that if the hinges have worn, they will allow the door to scrape its bottom edge on the sill as it is opened and closed. Result? Both door and sill scrape off paint, exposing metal and causing rust, quite apart from the surface wear through the friction contact of the two. As well as this, the front door post, the one upon which the hinges are hung, will bow and flex with the constant door movement, so you can finish up with a rippled, or even cracked, door hinge plate,

resulting in more weakening of the whole structure.

Most important of all, check the floor structure of your Alfasud or Sprint. If this is in sound condition, you can repair most other things, and as long as the front door/ windscreen pillars are solid, then you have a car which is worth the task of renovation. It is possible to obtain fibreglass panelwork for the Alfasud, but generally not thought a good idea. If you want to preserve your prized possession in a fully original form and you want to maintain its continuing valuation, then you have no alternative than to replace metal with metal. When you *have* replaced metal with metal, you will certainly want to preserve it for as long as possible. So take the advice which comes later under the heading of 'Rust and Restoration' and you stand a fair chance of keeping your car in one piece.

On the mechanical front, the Boxer engine has one major disadvantage, as the author found to his cost with a Sprint engine. Because there is a greater distance for the oil to travel to overhead camshafts, and because the flat-four's cams are opposite ends to each other, the oil takes a little longer to get there, so the owner needs to allow oil to travel all round the engine before revving it. A tell-tale tappet chatter from cold and on over-run will tell you that a previous owner has not been as careful as he or she might have, with the likely result of camshaft wear. Camshaft replacement is an expensive exercise, so check it carefully.

Check the oil pressure, watch for blue smoke on revving after several seconds tickover, which indicates worn or broken piston rings. And look for oil leaks, as well as checking the oil level before you buy. One very important item to check is the camshaft drive belts, since these are supposed to be replaced at every 36,000 miles (58,000km) and if they haven't been, then you could easily end up paying a lot of money for someone else's folly. It is always wise, if you can, to buy a car with a service history, since you can then often find out what you want to know if it isn't in front of you.

Now to the drive-train. Look for breaks in the rubber boots round the drive-joints, since splits could let in dust and cause terminal damage. Check the movement of springs, the condition of brake discs and look for free movement of calipers when applying the brakes. Inboard disc brakes have an awful habit of collecting mud and grit, so need regular service attention. As for the handbrake, it usually suffers from lack of lubrication and maintenance, which normally only presents itself as your car fails the annual test!

When you've checked all these things and decided that your car is mechanically and bodily sound, buy it while you can, because all too often good cars are snapped up quickly. And the Alfasud and Sprint *are* approaching the time for their values to rise. Almost certainly, the Sprint and TI will be first on the price-increase bandwagon, so be warned.

On the road, the Alfasud and Sprint are a delight to drive. In the author's experience, the driving position is slightly better than many of the rear-wheel-drive Alfas, simply because the steering wheel is in a slightly lower and flatter perspective than most rear-wheel-drive cars. It is the typical Italian short-leg long-arm situation, but if you prefer an upright sitting position anyway, that problem virtually disappears. If I have a criticism of the boxer-engined cars, it is that they are too low-geared for most road work. On the other hand, an Alfa Romeo engine is renowned for its capacity to rev, the high engine speed allowing quicker acceleration. However, the flat-four is not a particularly high torque engine, so you *have* to keep the engine speed high to extract the best from the car.

Whatever your complaints might be about miles-per-hour-per-thousand, the simple capacity to sit on a road and do what is asked of it is what makes the Alfasud and Sprint such interesting cars to drive. Their eventual emergence into motor sport testifies to this, since Alfasuds have acquitted themselves well both in racing and rallying. It is very difficult to persuade an Alfasud to lift two wheels from the ground and you have to be doing something pretty hairy to make the car do it. On the circuits, Alfasuds have out-performed other, far more expensive, small saloons and it would seem are capable of doing so on the road, too, as demonstrated by rallying.

For my money, if the choice comes down to a BMW 318 or an Alfa Romeo Sprint, then don't even ask yourself any more questions.

Just go out and buy the best Sprint you can find and afford.

FANCY THE ALFETTA?

One very major feature which recommends the Alfetta above *all* its adversaries is the fact the rear seat headroom is quite comfortable for most adults over long distances and no other coupe comes anywhere near this car in that respect. What's more, Signor Giugiaro managed to make the Alfetta GT Series still look like a sports car! Truth is, though, if you want one with a performance that comes anywhere near the looks of the car, you really *have* to go for a GTV2000/2.0 or a GTV6 2.5, because the later versions of Alfa Sprint will outperform the 1.6 or 1.8-engined Alfettas.

So what should you look for in your Alfetta? Well, again you must search out the rust patches and decide what you can best do with them. Again, look for the latest model you can possibly afford, though GTV6s are now going up in price by leaps and bounds, so don't take too long! The last 2.0s and 2.5s were quite well rust protected, but the six-year guarantee still doesn't prevent holes from appearing when you didn't expect them, so inspect the floorpan carefully and follow the screwdriver routine. Once more, check the windscreen area and the front wings, the usual little bubbles in the paint being the tell-tales. And again, check the inner wings as well as the outers and make sure the sills aren't too far gone. All of these things are replaceable but at a cost, and it's far better to take your time selecting the right car than letting yourself in for a huge bill.

As for the mechanical aspects of the Alfetta GTV, you need to check the propeller shaft couplings to be sure they are in good condition. If not, you may have the first sign that your dream car has been abused. If it has, then go no further, look for another car, because you could be in to high expense for gearbox/transaxle/driveshaft repairs. Remember also that the GTV6 has a twin-plate clutch to be checked. All in all, you may find it easier and more reassuring to get somebody who knows Alfas well, or even the AA, to check it over and look closely at all the potential problem areas. Then you buy your car!

Bearing in mind the changes in sports car tastes it is no longer necessary to buy an open car that freezes your single passenger out of existence. You *can* have four seats in your sports car without being ostracized. The proof of this is in the rapid appreciation of value of the Alfetta GTV cars, especially the GTV6 2.5. There is even one company rebuilding GTV6s for sale and offering the next best thing to a brand new one that you can buy now. For something in the order of £20,000, at the time of writing, you can buy a restructured GTV6, with totally rebuilt engine, including re-profiled camshafts to improve the car's performance, and all the other mechanical components renovated to give it new-car performance.

Such is the popularity of this superb car, that a certain German maker emulated the concept after many years with rear-engined cars (which actually were better) and offers a 2.5-litre version today which would still be hard pressed to outperform the Alfetta GTV6. Then, just to confound the world at large, there was a 3-litre version of the Alfetta built in South Africa, fitted with carburettors (along the lines of the original Alfa Six Saloon), and producing 190-plus brake horsepower. Leading Alfa racer and enthusiast, Jon Dooley, brought one into Britain in 1987 and Gordon Cruickshank, of *Motor Sport* eulogized over its performance for weeks after trying it out.

THE METAL RESTORATION JOB

Restoring any Alfa has to be a labour of love.

That is, you have to love the car and be willing to labour over it long and hard. If you meet these two important criteria, then you are on the way to owning one of the most enjoyable cars of realistic value in modern times. As a bonus, modern 'classic' Alfa Romeos are also now beginning to be appreciated as assets, so the car investor is starting to show interest, which will inevitably have an effect on the ultimate values of these thoroughly fun cars.

Whatever Alfa you have picked, though, is ultimately going to need an amount of metal work and when you see signs of deterioration you must accept that the sooner you tackle it, the less expensive and less arduous it will be to deal with. It may sound drastic, but the best way to deal with the rust-bug is to cut the paint right back to the metal – or body filler. Too many 'nice-looking' cars have carried a bonus of 7lb of body filler! And body filler is no substitute for metal, since eventually it will just fall out as the body rots further round the hole the filler filled.

When you've stripped the paint off, you may well have a much lighter-weight car than you expected – peppered with rust holes in the lower regions! But don't despair, it's almost certainly curable. It is the experience of most who know far more about recovering Alfa Romeos than I, that the basic structure of all the Alfas we're talking of here is usually sound enough to sustain restoration. It goes without saying that if you have major panelwork to repair or replace, it will be beyond the skill of most amateurs, so you need to pick a professional who can be trusted to do a workmanlike job without taking you, the impoverished enthusiast, to the cleaners. The best advice in this situation is to contact your local Alfa Romeo club, because there will always be someone who can tell who *not* to entrust with your favourite car, which is probably your life savings, too. The process of major surgery on your beloved Alfa need not then be too traumatic.

PREVENTION IS BETTER THAN CURE

When you've removed *all* the paint from your beloved Alfa and the rust-damaged metal has been repaired, you presumably will want to prevent the same awful fate befalling your pride and joy again for as long as possible? Then consider these steps in long-term care. Firstly, make sure that the car is *completely* dry, inside and out, then drill every box-section in the whole structure and inject it with either Waxoyl or some other form of long-term rust inhibitor. Normally, plastic plugs then fill the holes you have drilled and the metal is protected on the inside.

Having taken the best steps you can to prevent rust from coming out from the inside, you now need to protect those awkward nooks and crannies that most manufacturers build into their products in the process of pressing those folds and turns we like to call 'styling features'. This is best done by ensuring that liberal amounts of rust-preventive priming coat is applied in those obscure regions, followed by a waxing to protect against the effects of condensation, which is one of the worst metal killers known to motorists. After this, apply the *minimum necessary* body filler, to take out small deformations, followed by a couple of coats of rust-inhibitive primer, such as zinc chromate, rubbing down carefully between each coat.

Choosing and applying the finish colour is as important as rubbing down the bodywork to bare metal in the first place, since this has as much to do with protecting the car as everything you've done so far. Polyurethane paints are quite flexible and can sustain stone-chips, the bane of most paint-jobs, quite well. Two-pack finishes can also give a superb finish and be durable. But always make sure you have a colour sample applied to a metal panel which has been treated the same way as your car, to guarantee the best colour match you can achieve. Remember

*A very attractive and original
1975 Spider 2000.*

though, the finished surface will only ever give as deep a gloss finish as your preparation work will have allowed.

THE MECHANICAL RENOVATION

I'm only going to give a few recommendations here, since, if you want a complete overhaul, you will in most cases take the engine to an Alfa Romeo expert, checking out the best recommendations of your local Alfa Romeo club before entrusting it to anyone. Then, even with the most trusted expert, for your own satisfaction and for the sake of preparing yourself for the worst, always ensure that you obtain a full condition report from the expert and agree a schedule of work to be carried out. It *should* be right when you get it back, but at the end of the day, at least you have *some* recourse, however meagre, under a rebuilder's guarantee. You can't guarantee your own workmanship, so if you're not sure, then don't.

If you *do* decide to strip an engine yourself, always make copious notes of the dismantling procedure, because to follow it in reverse will help ensure you leave nothing out and will simply help you get it back together if you've not taken one of its kind apart before. Check, and mark if you have to, the timing positions of crankshaft and camshafts, before dismantling. Always make sure that the engine components you intend to use in re-assembly are clean and free from grit. *Never ever* re-fit old shell bearings, even if they look perfectly serviceable and the surfaces they have supported are well within tolerances of wear and roundness. Because you will *never* be able to put those bearings back the way they came out of the engine. So, for the sake of a little cost, replace them.

Gearboxes and final drives are another area where great care has to be exercised in renovation. And again, if you are not *fully* conversant with the job requiring to be done, the best advise you can have is: don't do it. Call in an expert and pay for the work to be done properly. That way, you'll have far better peace of mind when it comes to driving, especially if you plan to drive the car as it was designed to be driven. All in all, the best possible advice you can be given as you set out to buy the Alfa of your choice is: 'Join the Club'. And welcome to the world of *Alfisti*.

At this point, the old myth of Henry Ford comes to mind, for it is he who said, according to a motor industry legend: 'When I see an Alfa Romeo, I raise my hat'. Donald Petersen, Ford's Chief Executive when that company was trying to acquire the interests of Alfa Romeo in 1986, certainly was ready to raise *his* hat to Alfa Romeo – and did so in the process of making his company's unsuccessful bid for this great Italian name. That is respect indeed – and respect deserved for a car which became and has been for many years a legend in its own time.

Appendices

Appendix 1(a)   Alfa Romeo Production Numbers – The Spider Series*

ALFA ROMEO MODEL	1955	1956	1957	1958	1959	1960	1961	1962	1963	1964	1965	1966	TOTAL
Giulietta/Giulia Spyder/ Spyder Veloce	1	1,021	2,192	2,386	2,224	5,094	3,169	1,182	4,241	3,175	801	3,627	**29,113**

ALFA ROMEO MODEL	1967	1968	1969	1970	1971	1972	1973	1974	1975	1976	1977	1978	TOTAL
Spider Duetto 1600	2,958			1									2,959
Giulia Spider 1600						928							928
1750 Spider Veloce	854	18	915	657	592								3,036
1750 Spider Veloce RHD		209	286	2	135								632
1750 Spider Veloce USA		259	1,146	1,426	1,211	7	2						4,051
Giulia Spider 1300 Junior		1,743	760	542	749	806							4,600
Spider 1300 Junior RHD		97	82										179
2000 Spider Veloce					733								733
2000 Spider Veloce RHD					78								78
2000 Spider Veloce USA					12	11							23
Spider 2000 (133bhp)					823	2,905	1,418	1,002	580	424	216		7,368
Spider 2000 (128bhp)									770	728	1,035	1,008	3,541
Spider 2.0 USA							1,419	3,242	2,606	2,510	2,315	2,342	14,434
Spider 1600 Junior (109bhp)							1,010	231	202				1,443
Spider 1600 Junior (102bhp)								104	330	344	300	567	1,645
Production Totals	3,812	2,326	3,189	2,628	4,333	4,657	3,849	4,579	4,488	4,006	3,866	3,917	**45,650**

ALFA ROMEO MODEL	1979	1980	1981	1982	1983	1984	1985	1986	1987	1988	1989	1990	TOTAL
Spider 1600 Junior (102bhp)	269	366	204										839
Spider 1.6					1,293	605	605	728	352	822	995	971	6,371
Spider 2000 (128bhp)	1,275	3,221	708	207									5,411
Spider 2.0				92	2,336	2,231	1,375	6,287	4,295	3,349	3,000	6,135	29,100
Spider 2.0 USA	2,699	1,797	524	1,975	2,624	5,872	2,656						18,147
Spider 2.0 Veloce USA							1,511						1,511
Spider 2.0 Quad Verde							1						1
Spider 2.0 USA Quad Verde							653						653
Production Totals	4,243	5,384	1,436	2,274	6,253	8,708	6,801	7,015	4,647	4,171	3,995	7,106	**62,033**

* Including Giuletta, Giulia, Duetto, 1750 and 2000.

Appendix 1(b) The Alfasud Saloons

ALFA ROMEO MODEL	1972	1973	1974	1975	1976	1977	1978	1979	1980	1981	1982	1983	1984	1985	TOTAL
Alfasud (Basic model)	21,057	77,322	71,609	9,432	24										179,444
Alfasud TI 1200		1,575	28,159	21,884	26,748	10,361							4		88,731
Alfasud N			262	12,892	5,720	7,794	10,999	8,754	4	1					46,426
Alfasud L				46,952	57,138	48,286	91						1		152,468
Alfasud Super 1.2						2,863	21,662	25,439	4						49,968
Alfasud Super 1.2 (Srs 3)									33,496	33,715	12,267	13	2		79,493
Alfasud Super 1.3						6,843	21,997								28,840
Alfasud Super 1.5							2,859	16,543	5						19,407
Alfasud Super 1.5 (Srs 3)									15,030	10,029	2,634		2		27,695
Alfasud Super 1350							6,305	11,652	6	1					17,964
Alfasud Super 1350 (Srs 3)									18,740	13,244	5,560				37,544
Alfasud TI 1.3						9,000	6,068								15,068
Alfasud TI 1350							4,129	4,864	109						9,102
Alfasud TI 1350 (Srs 3)									3,469	802					4,271
Alfasud TI 1.5							11,459	15,848	1,904						29,211
Alfasud TI 1.5 (Srs 3)									6,900	2,722					9,622
Alfasud Valentino 1.2									1,589	630					2,219
Alfasud Valentino 1350									3	895					898
Alfasud Valentino 1.5									4	868					872
Alfasud Base (1982 only)											2,279				2,279
Alfasud 1.2 3-Door Hatchback										4,446	227		1		4,674
Alfasud 1.2 5-Door Hatchback											13,581	7,002	4		20,587
Alfasud 1350 3-Door										4,272	3,888	494	5		8,659
Alfasud 1350 5-Door											9,910	1,159			11,069
Alfasud 1.5 3-Door Hatchback										4,182	1,453	160			5,795
Alfasud 1.5 5-Dr Quadr Oro											9,768	2,026			11,794
Alfasud TI 1350 3-Door										2,808	2,038	1,338	40	16	6,240
Alfasud TI 1.5 3-Door										7,714	6,564	8			14,286
Alfasud TI 1.5 3-Dr Quad Verde											2,798	6,295			9,093
Production Totals	21,057	78,897	100,030	91,160	89,630	85,147	85,569	83,100	81,263	86,329	72,967	18,495	59	16	893,719

Appendix 1(c) – The Alfetta GTs, Alfasud Sprint and Alfa Romeo Sprint Series

ALFA ROMEO MODEL	1974	1975	1976	1977	1978	1979	1980	1981	1982	1983	1984	1985	1986	1987	1988	1989	TOTAL
Alfetta GT 1800 (121bhp)	6,400	10,332	876														17,608
Alfetta GT 1800 (115bhp)		1,642															1,642
Alfetta GT 1.8			2,657														2,657
Alfetta GT 1600			4,262														4,262
Alfetta GT 1.6				7,935	3,321	787	618										12,661
Alfetta GTV 2000			11,210	14,359													25,569
Alfetta GTV 2000 USA		1,942	3,314	442													5,698
Alfetta GTV 2.0L					10,699	8,008	4,055	3	174	4,142	2,011	762	207				30,061
Alfetta GTV 2.0 USA L					2,058	1,281	4										3,343
Alfetta GTV6 2.5						2	1,178	4,533	3,619	3,605	2,403	1,653	686				17,679
Alfetta GTV6 2.5 USA							1	1,272	1,116	513	1,050	722					4,674
Alfetta GTV6 2.5 Catalyst												28					28
Alfetta GTV6 3.0 (RSA)														200			200
Production Totals	6,400	13,916	22,319	22,736	16,078	10,078	5,856	5,808	4,909	8,260	5,464	3,165	893	200			126,082
Alfasud Sprint 1.3			2,192	12,046	4,118												18,356
Alfasud Sprint Veloce 1.3							2,000	1,060	741								3,801
Alfasud Sprint 1.3 (Srs 3)										2,754	1,176	7					3,937
Alfasud Sprint 1.3 (2a)											235	866	667	450	811	8	3,037
Alfasud Sprint 1350					1,164	1,675											2,839
Alfasud Sprint 1.5					14,414	11,287	122										25,823
Alfasud Sprint Veloce 1.5							13,854	7,846	10,042	192							31,934
Alfasud Sprint Plus 1.5								2,003	4								2,007
Alfasud Sprint Saloon 1.5									250								250
Alfa Romeo Sprint 1.5 (Srs 3)										2,049	432	3					2,484
Alfa Romeo Sprint 1.5 2a												262					262
Alfa Romeo Sprint 1.5 Quad Verde										9,695	3,248	22					12,965
Alfa Romeo Sprint 1.5 Quad Verde 2a											577	2,778	3,063	2,400			8,818
Alfa Romeo Sprint 1.7														663	4,212	46	4,921
Alfa Romeo Sprint 1.7 Veloce																	
Production Totals			2,192	12,046	19,696	12,962	15,976	10,909	11,037	14,690	5,668	3,938	3,730	3,513	5,023	54	121,434

Appendix 2   Alfa Romeo Clubs Around the World

AUSTRALIA

Alfa Romeo Owners' Club of Australia
PO Box 216
Camberwell
Victoria 3124

CANADA

Alfa Romeo Club de Canada
PO Box 62
Station Q
Toronto
Ontario
M4T 2L7

FRANCE

Alfa Romeo Club de France
Bastarous
Chemin des Crêtes
64290 Gan

GREAT BRITAIN

The Alfa Romeo Owners' Club
97 High Street
Linton
Cambridge
CB1 6JT

NEW ZEALAND

Alfa Romeo Owners' Club of New Zealand
33 Gray Avenue
Paraparaumu Beach
New Zealand

SOUTH AFRICA

Cape Alfa Romeo Club RSA
PO Box 804
Belleville 7530
Capetown

SWITZERLAND

Registre Suisse Alfa Romeo
Case Postale 196
1000 Lausanne 12

UNITED STATES OF AMERICA

The Alfa Romeo Owners' Club
2304 San Pasqual Valley Road
Escondido
California 92027

Index